MathFlare

Name: ___________________________

Class: ___________

Teacher: ___________________________

Introduction

As parents and educators, we recognize the pivotal role mathematics plays in shaping a child's academic journey and future success. Yet, the path to mathematical proficiency can often seem daunting, fraught with challenges and complexities. That's where the transformative power of MathFlare Workbooks shine through, illuminating the way forward with clarity, precision, and purpose.

Introducing MathFlare Workbooks – a beacon of guidance, a testament to excellence, and a catalyst for achievement. Crafted with meticulous care and expertise, MathFlare Workbooks stand as paragons of educational excellence, designed to nurture young minds, ignite a passion for learning, and develop a deep-rooted understanding of mathematical concepts.

Picture this: your child eagerly delves into the pages of Mathflare Workbook, greeted by a step-by-step guide illuminated with vivid examples that demystify complex mathematical concepts. With each turn of the page, they embark on a journey of discovery, encountering thoughtfully curated practice questions that reinforce learning and hone problem-solving skills. And when they unveil the answers to those very questions, a sense of accomplishment blossoms within them – a tangible reward for their hard work and dedication.

But MathFlare Workbooks are more than just tools for learning; they are pathways to comprehension, fostering a deep-seated understanding of mathematical concepts through a sequential, logical flow. From fundamental principles to advanced problem-solving strategies, every chapter builds upon the last, ensuring a robust foundation upon which future knowledge can be constructed.

As parents, we yearn for nothing more than to see our children thrive, to witness the spark of inspiration ignited within them as they conquer academic challenges with confidence and poise. MathFlare Workbooks serve as partners in this noble endeavor, offering not just practice questions, but the keys to unlocking a world of opportunity.

And for teachers, MathFlare Workbooks stand as invaluable allies in the quest to cultivate mathematical proficiency in the classroom. With answers readily available, instructors can focus on guiding and nurturing their students, confident in the knowledge that MathFlare Workbooks provide a solid framework upon which to build.

In the pages of MathFlare Workbooks, we find not just the promise of academic excellence, but the seeds of a brighter tomorrow. So let us embrace the power of mathematics, let us champion the journey of learning, and let us pave the way for a generation of young minds poised to shape the world. With MathFlare Workbooks as our guide, the possibilities are infinite, and the future, bright.

Table of Contents

MathFlare
MATH WORKBOOK
Grade 2
Step by Step Guide and Essential Practice with Answers
Addition Subtraction
Multiplication
Place Value and Expanded Notations
Geometry
MathFlare Publishing

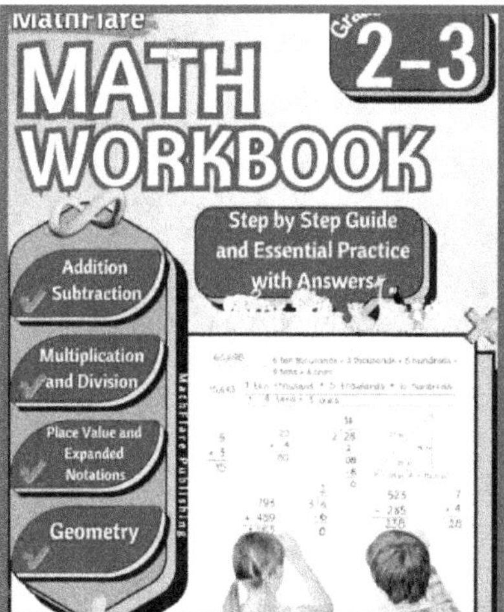
MathFlare
MATH WORKBOOK
Grade 2-3
Step by Step Guide and Essential Practice with Answers
Addition Subtraction
Multiplication and Division
Place Value and Expanded Notations
Geometry
MathFlare Publishing

MathFlare
MATH WORKBOOK
Grade 3
Step by Step Guide and Essential Practice with Answers
Multiplication and Division
Decimals
Place Value and Expanded Notations
Fractions and Geometry
MathFlare Publishing

MathFlare
MATH WORKBOOK
Grade 1
Step by Step Guide and Essential Practice with Answers
Counting and Numbers
Addition and Subtraction
Place Value and Expanded Notations
Understanding Time
MathFlare Publishing

MathFlare
MATH WORKBOOK
Grade 1-2
Step by Step Guide and Essential Practice with Answers
Counting and Numbers
Addition and Subtraction
Place Value and Expanded Notations
Understanding Time
MathFlare Publishing

MathFlare
MATH WORKBOOK
Grade 3-4
Step by Step Guide and Essential Practice with Answers
Addition Subtraction
Multiplication Division
Place Value and Expanded Notations
Fractions and Geometry
MathFlare Publishing

MathFlare
MATH WORKBOOK
Grade 4
Step by Step Guide and Essential Practice with Answers
Addition Subtraction
Multiplication Division
Place Value and Expanded Notations
Fractions and Geometry
MathFlare Publishing

MathFlare
MATH WORKBOOK
Grade 4-5
Step by Step Guide and Essential Practice with Answers
Multiplication Division
Place Value and Expanded Notations
Fractions and Geometry
Unit Conversion
MathFlare Publishing

MathFlare
Grade 5
MATH WORKBOOK
Step by Step Guide and Essential Practice with Answers
Multiplication Division
Place Value and Expanded Notations
Fractions and Geometry
Unit Conversion
MathFlare Publishing

MathFlare
Grade 5-6
MATH WORKBOOK
Step by Step Guide and Essential Practice with Answers
Multiplication Division
Place Value and Expanded Notations
Fractions and Geometry
Units and Statistics
MathFlare Publishing

MathFlare
Grade 6
MATH WORKBOOK
Step by Step Guide and Essential Practice with Answers
Integers and Statistics
Arithmetic and Pre-Algebra
Fractions and Geometry
Ratio and Percentage
MathFlare Publishing

MathFlare
Grade 6-7
MATH WORKBOOK
Step by Step Guide and Essential Practice with Answers
Arithmetic and Pre-Algebra
Ratio, Percent Proportion
Geometry
Statistics
MathFlare Publishing

MathFlare
Grade 7
MATH WORKBOOK
Step by Step Guide and Essential Practice with Answers
Pre-Algebra
Ratio, Percent Proportion
Geometry
Statistics
MathFlare Publishing

MathFlare
Grade 7-8
MATH WORKBOOK
Step by Step Guide and Essential Practice with Answers
Pre-Algebra
Ratio, Percent Proportion
Geometry and Cartesian Plane
Statistics
MathFlare Publishing

MathFlare
Grade 8-9
MATH WORKBOOK
Step by Step Guide and Essential Practice with Answers
Pre-Algebra
Ratio, Proportion and Percentage
Linear Equations
Geometry and Cartesian Plane
MathFlare Publishing

MathFlare
Grade 8
MATH WORKBOOK
Step by Step Guide and Essential Practice with Answers
Pre-Algebra
Percentage
Linear Equations
Geometry
MathFlare Publishing

Addition and Subtraction

Addition with Regrouping

When we do addition, we combine numbers. But sometimes, when we're adding numbers, we might need to regroup. Regrouping means we have to move a number from one place to another, usually to the next column, to get the right answer.

For Example: Let's take an example of adding 533 and 579 together:

$$\begin{array}{r} 5\ 3\ 3 \\ +\ \underline{5\ 7\ 9} \end{array}$$

First, we start by adding the digits in the ones place: 3 + 9 = 12. We write down the 2 in the ones place and carry over the 1 to the tens place.

$$\begin{array}{r} 1 \\ 5\ 3\ 3 \\ +\ \underline{5\ 7\ 9} \\ 2 \end{array}$$

Now, we add the digits in the tens place, along with the carry-over: 2 + 8 + 1 = 11. We write down the 1 in the tens place and carry over the 1 to the hundreds place.

$$\begin{array}{r} 1\ 1 \\ 5\ 2\ 2 \\ +\ \underline{5\ 8\ 9} \\ 1\ 2 \end{array}$$

Now, we add the digits in the hundreds place, along with the carry-over: 5 + 5 + 1 = 11. We write down the 1 in the tens place and carry over the 1 to the hundreds place.

$$\begin{array}{r} 1\ 1 \\ 5\ 2\ 2 \\ +\ 5\ 8\ 9 \\ \hline 1\ 1\ 1\ 2 \end{array}$$

This process of carrying over helps us accurately add numbers, especially when they're larger.

Subtraction with Regrouping

Subtraction is a key math operation where we find the difference between two numbers. Sometimes, when we subtract, we might need to regroup, which means borrowing from the next column.

Let's take an example of subtracting 436 from 563:

First, we start by subtracting the digits in the ones place: 3 - 6.

Since 3 is less than 6, we need to regroup. We borrow 1 from the tens place, making it 5 tens instead of 6, and add it to the ones place.

So, 3 becomes 13, and then we subtract 6.

$$\begin{array}{r} 5\ \ 6\ \ {}_{1}3 \\ -\ 4\ \ 3\ \ 6 \\ \hline 7 \end{array}$$

Now, we subtract the tens place digits: 5 - 3 = 2

$$\begin{array}{r} 5 \\ 5\ \ \cancel{6}\,{}_{1}3 \\ -\ 4\ \ 3\ \ 6 \\ \hline 2\ \ 7 \end{array}$$

Now, we subtract the hundreds place digits: 5 - 4 = 1

$$
\begin{array}{r}
5 \\
5\ \ \cancel{6}\ {}_1 3 \\
-\ 4\ \ 3\ \ 6 \\
\hline
1\ \ 2\ \ 7
\end{array}
$$

This process of regrouping or borrowing helps us accurately subtract numbers, especially when the top digit is smaller than the bottom one.

Let's solve problems from exercises:

$$
\begin{array}{r}
793 \\
+\ 459 \\
\hline
1{,}252 \\
\hline
\end{array}
\qquad
\begin{array}{r}
523 \\
-\ 285 \\
\hline
238 \\
\hline
\end{array}
$$

Word Problems

Word problems are like little puzzles that help us use addition in real-life situations.

For instance:

1. Jake has 6 carrots. He gets 2 more carrots. How many carrots does he have now?

To find out how many carrots he has now, we add the number of carrots he started with (6) to the number of carrots he got (2).

So, we add 6 + 2, which equals 8. Jake now has 8 carrots in total!

2. Jake saved up 4 dollars to buy pencils. He spent 2 dollars on it. How much money does he have left?

To solve this problem, we need to start with the number of dollars Jake started with and subtract the number of dollars he spent on the pencils.

So, we subtract 2 from 4, which equals 2: Jake has 2 dollars left after buying the pencils.

We need to understand what the problem is asking and what information it provides. Then, we can use addition or subtraction, depending on whether we're combining or taking away objects, to find the answer.

Let's solve problems from exercises:

Alice rode a horse for 8 miles yesterday and 16 miles today. In total, how many miles did she ride?

$$
\begin{array}{r}
8 \\
+\ 16 \\
\hline
24
\end{array}
\qquad
\begin{array}{l}
\text{Alice rode 8 miles yesterday} \\
\text{She rode 16 miles today} \\
\text{She rode 24 miles in total}
\end{array}
$$

There are 2 calculators in a bag. Samantha took 2 calculators   out of the bag. How many calculators are still in the bag?

$$
\begin{array}{r}
2 \\
-\ 2 \\
\hline
0
\end{array}
\qquad
\begin{array}{l}
\text{there are 2 calculators in the bag} \\
\text{Samantha took 2 calculators} \\
\text{there are 0 calculators in the bag}
\end{array}
$$

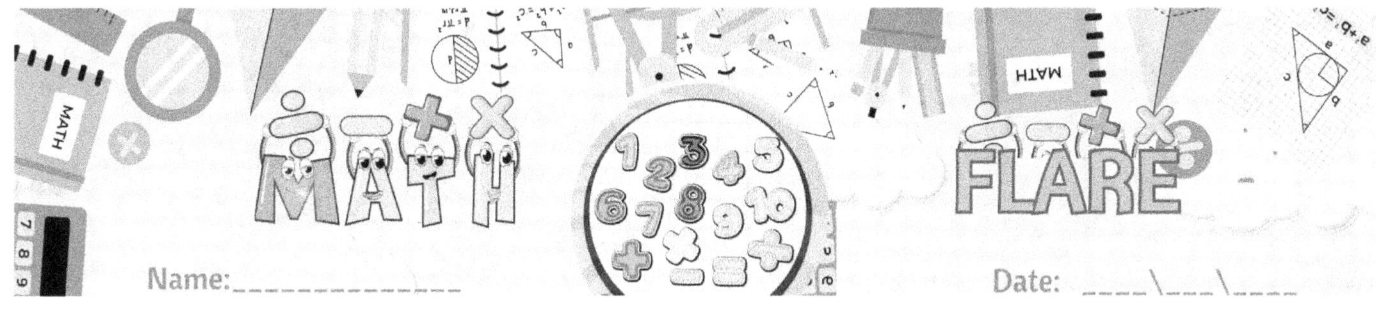

Name:___________________   Date: _____________

Addition with Regrouping

Find the sum.

1. 823 + 599	2. 811 + 399	3. 215 + 899	4. 325 + 898
5. 498 + 957	6. 411 + 799	7. 24 + 696	8. 356 + 789
9. 59 + 665	10. 226 + 985	11. 818 + 397	12. 211 + 899
13. 337 + 779	14. 559 + 776	15. 745 + 799	16. 748 + 796
17. 921 + 499	18. 162 + 979	19. 581 + 889	20. 341 + 899

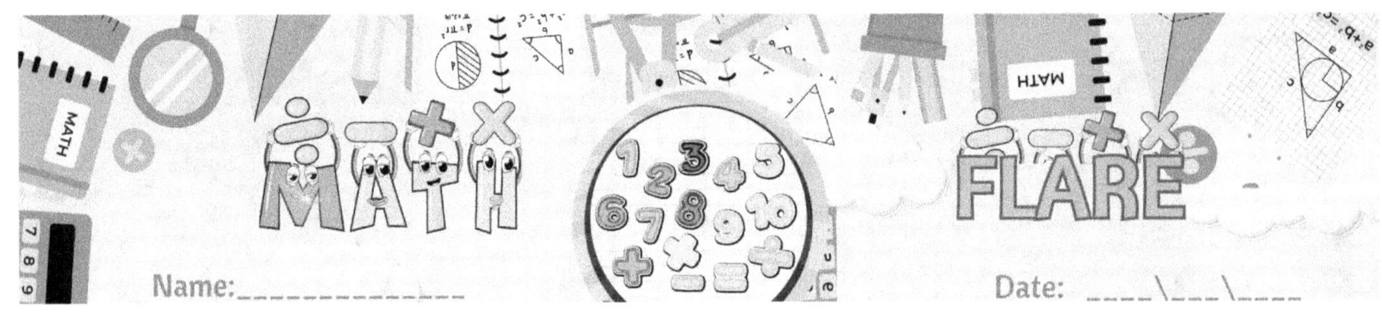

21. 988 + 728	22. 387 + 745	23. 799 + 942	24. 494 + 869
25. 77 + 259	26. 274 + 859	27. 397 + 835	28. 212 + 999
29. 345 + 767	30. 49 + 995	31. 911 + 99	32. 573 + 758
33. 619 + 694	34. 831 + 579	35. 442 + 788	36. 111 + 999
37. 286 + 867	38. 157 + 84	39. 799 + 756	40. 856 + 396

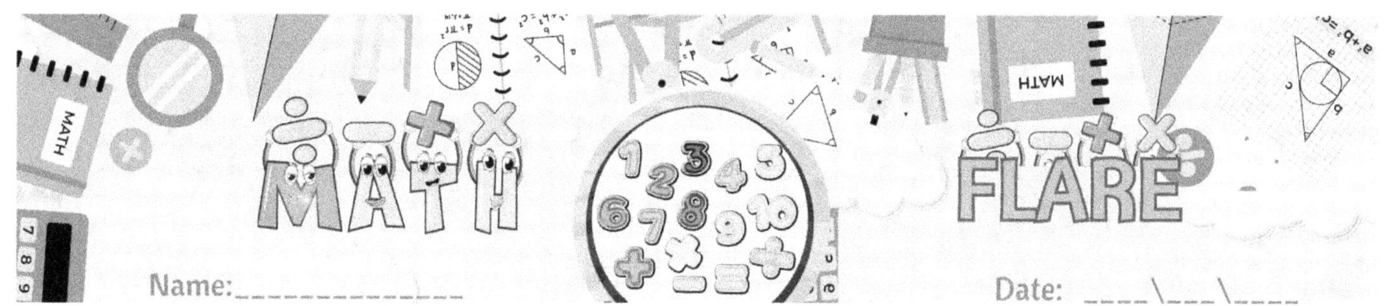

41. 785 + 998	42. 194 + 987	43. 471 + 899	44. 244 + 997
45. 831 + 489	46. 134 + 986	47. 559 + 974	48. 156 + 975
49. 836 + 986	50. 113 + 997	51. 121 + 999	52. 159 + 998
53. 571 + 649	54. 978 + 132	55. 838 + 589	56. 311 + 799
57. 151 + 959	58. 862 + 88	59. 285 + 875	60. 214 + 96

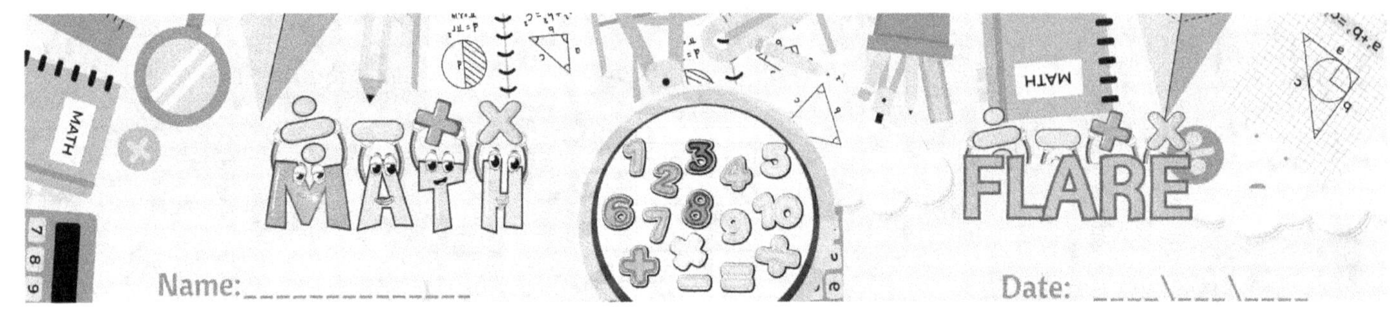

61. 327 + 998	62. 353 + 877	63. 743 + 888	64. 219 + 893
65. 924 + 198	66. 921 + 689	67. 284 + 867	68. 881 + 299
69. 329 + 94	70. 325 + 788	71. 819 + 292	72. 686 + 945
73. 124 + 989	74. 255 + 858	75. 73 + 77	76. 348 + 882
77. 972 + 69	78. 599 + 562	79. 543 + 789	80. 655 + 689

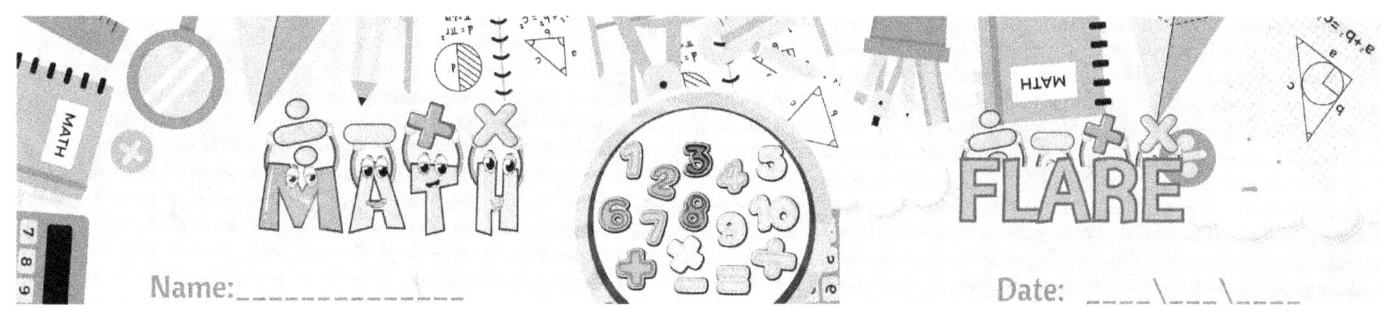

81. 421 + 789	82. 218 + 998	83. 669 + 677	84. 371 + 999
85. 23 + 599	86. 757 + 783	87. 391 + 849	88. 236 + 885
89. 232 + 989	90. 554 + 568	91. 626 + 584	92. 152 + 958
93. 819 + 798	94. 699 + 916	95. 263 + 978	96. 756 + 867
97. 419 + 696	98. 352 + 59	99. 914 + 96	100. 573 + 897

101. 636 + 599	102. 314 + 996	103. 732 + 589	104. 832 + 389
105. 971 + 439	106. 928 + 393	107. 64 + 869	108. 615 + 497
109. 852 + 878	110. 931 + 189	111. 29 + 384	112. 818 + 996
113. 794 + 758	114. 92 + 189	115. 311 + 899	116. 539 + 92
117. 153 + 967	118. 916 + 699	119. 541 + 689	120. 68 + 176

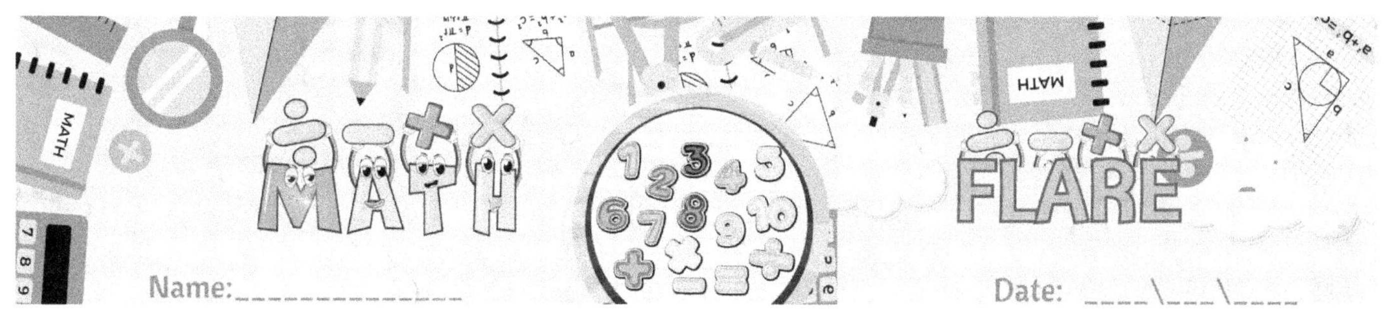

121. 384 + 878	122. 718 + 395	123. 919 + 97	124. 574 + 987
125. 451 + 959	126. 165 + 958	127. 562 + 959	128. 936 + 295
129. 711 + 499	130. 343 + 977	131. 438 + 696	132. 74 + 757
133. 893 + 867	134. 241 + 899	135. 953 + 967	136. 812 + 999
137. 814 + 799	138. 772 + 559	139. 636 + 485	140. 992 + 768

141. 182 + 989	142. 733 + 797	143. 53 + 897	144. 511 + 699
145. 726 + 695	146. 942 + 189	147. 343 + 98	148. 733 + 799
149. 815 + 996	150. 431 + 79	151. 787 + 673	152. 531 + 689
153. 739 + 996	154. 899 + 871	155. 185 + 987	156. 656 + 787
157. 412 + 798	158. 797 + 828	159. 917 + 395	160. 712 + 98

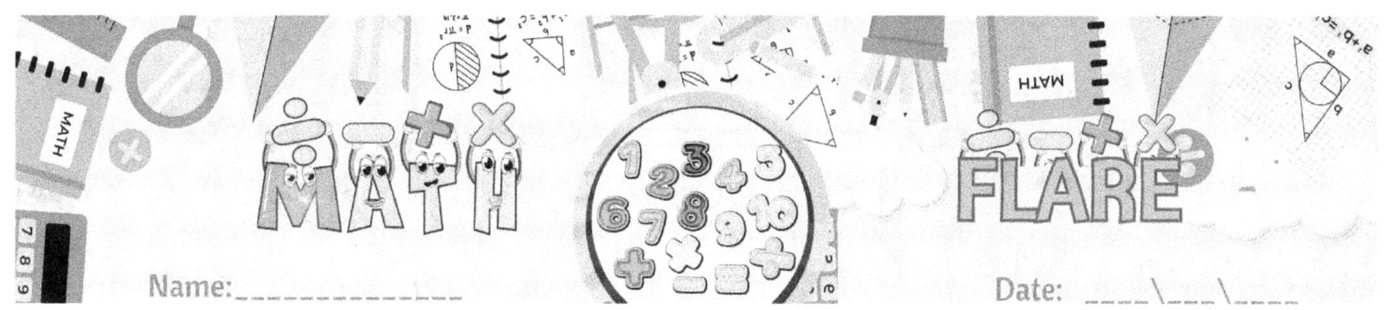

Name: ___________________________   Date: _____ \ _____ \ _____

161. 368 + 44	162. 676 + 469	163. 21 + 699	164. 826 + 794
165. 29 + 98	166. 346 + 889	167. 54 + 967	168. 981 + 49
169. 81 + 249	170. 21 + 99	171. 938 + 699	172. 14 + 999
173. 969 + 786	174. 727 + 787	175. 294 + 927	176. 816 + 497
177. 252 + 879	178. 685 + 745	179. 497 + 696	180. 468 + 66

Name:________________ Date: ____________

181. 171 + 989	182. 773 + 549	183. 442 + 979	184. 164 + 976
185. 594 + 787	186. 748 + 672	187. 294 + 946	188. 121 + 989
189. 31 + 789	190. 361 + 999	191. 947 + 67	192. 422 + 698
193. 224 + 897	194. 431 + 689	195. 256 + 888	196. 514 + 899
197. 779 + 956	198. 886 + 754	199. 926 + 888	200. 498 + 995

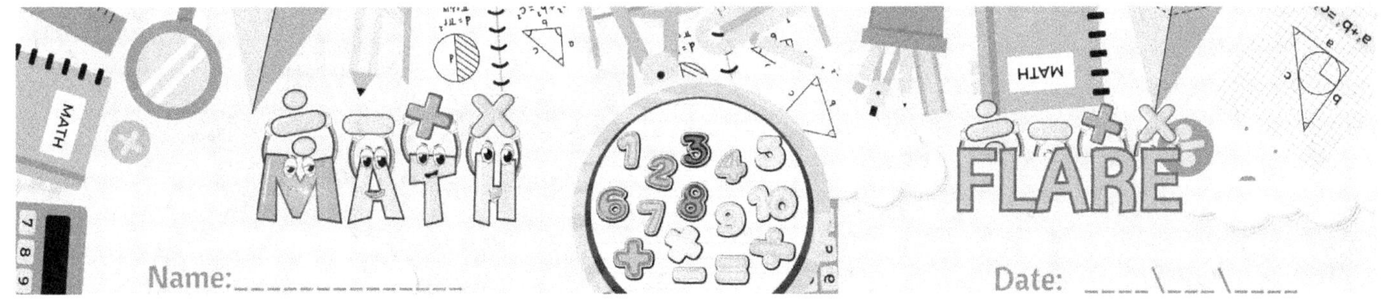

Subtraction with Regrouping

Find the difference.

201.	606 − 158	202.	256 − 199	203.	240 − 56	204.	278 − 199
205.	328 − 9	206.	741 − 563	207.	856 − 169	208.	206 − 29
209.	786 − 598	210.	928 − 549	211.	588 − 299	212.	284 − 195
213.	446 − 387	214.	903 − 336	215.	783 − 297	216.	767 − 189

217. $\begin{array}{r} 315 \\ -\ 178 \\ \hline \end{array}$	218. $\begin{array}{r} 757 \\ -\ 568 \\ \hline \end{array}$	219. $\begin{array}{r} 986 \\ -\ 899 \\ \hline \end{array}$	220. $\begin{array}{r} 970 \\ -\ 97 \\ \hline \end{array}$
221. $\begin{array}{r} 680 \\ -\ 592 \\ \hline \end{array}$	222. $\begin{array}{r} 482 \\ -\ 196 \\ \hline \end{array}$	223. $\begin{array}{r} 572 \\ -\ 497 \\ \hline \end{array}$	224. $\begin{array}{r} 134 \\ -\ 86 \\ \hline \end{array}$
225. $\begin{array}{r} 854 \\ -\ 665 \\ \hline \end{array}$	226. $\begin{array}{r} 980 \\ -\ 296 \\ \hline \end{array}$	227. $\begin{array}{r} 951 \\ -\ 865 \\ \hline \end{array}$	228. $\begin{array}{r} 507 \\ -\ 48 \\ \hline \end{array}$
229. $\begin{array}{r} 236 \\ -\ 167 \\ \hline \end{array}$	230. $\begin{array}{r} 308 \\ -\ 89 \\ \hline \end{array}$	231. $\begin{array}{r} 326 \\ -\ 288 \\ \hline \end{array}$	232. $\begin{array}{r} 860 \\ -\ 795 \\ \hline \end{array}$
233. $\begin{array}{r} 346 \\ -\ 197 \\ \hline \end{array}$	234. $\begin{array}{r} 567 \\ -\ 279 \\ \hline \end{array}$	235. $\begin{array}{r} 488 \\ -\ 299 \\ \hline \end{array}$	236. $\begin{array}{r} 303 \\ -\ 257 \\ \hline \end{array}$

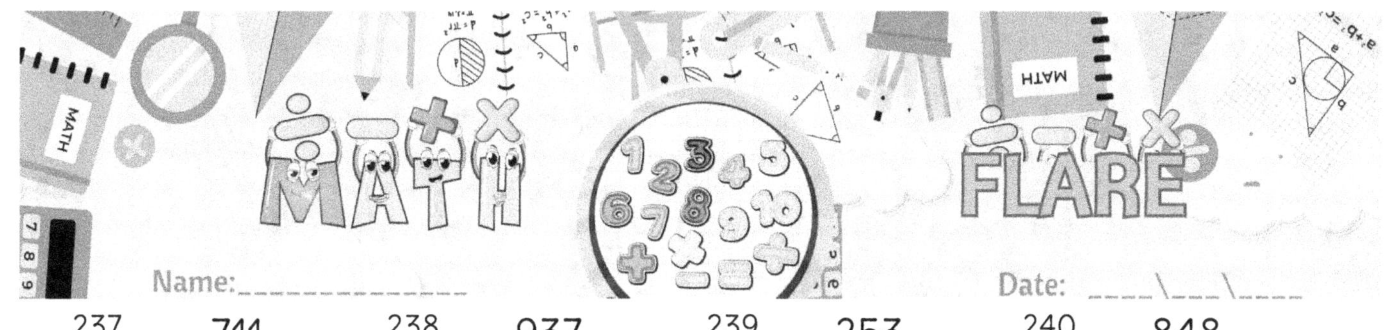

237.	238.	239.	240.
711 − 652	937 − 679	253 − 178	848 − 489

241.	242.	243.	244.
848 − 279	648 − 599	437 − 279	284 − 98

245.	246.	247.	248.
918 − 599	686 − 98	715 − 487	844 − 677

249.	250.	251.	252.
981 − 596	968 − 899	311 − 175	246 − 157

253.	254.	255.	256.
583 − 95	637 − 68	980 − 791	118 − 9

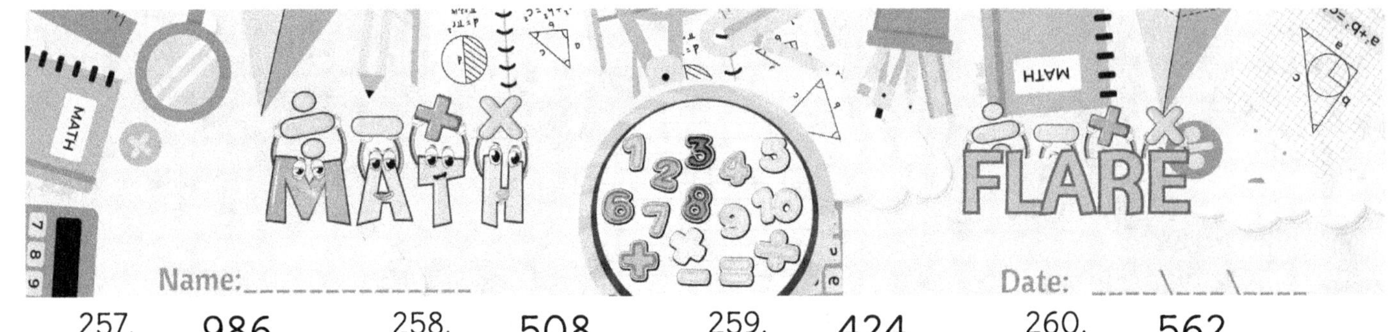

Name:________________   Date: ____________

257.	258.	259.	260.
986 - 799	508 - 499	424 - 369	562 - 495

261.	262.	263.	264.
401 - 77	608 - 489	786 - 197	348 - 259

265.	266.	267.	268.
114 - 96	763 - 497	111 - 95	357 - 98

269.	270.	271.	272.
213 - 28	484 - 196	878 - 189	416 - 77

273.	274.	275.	276.
666 - 397	275 - 186	303 - 268	482 - 95

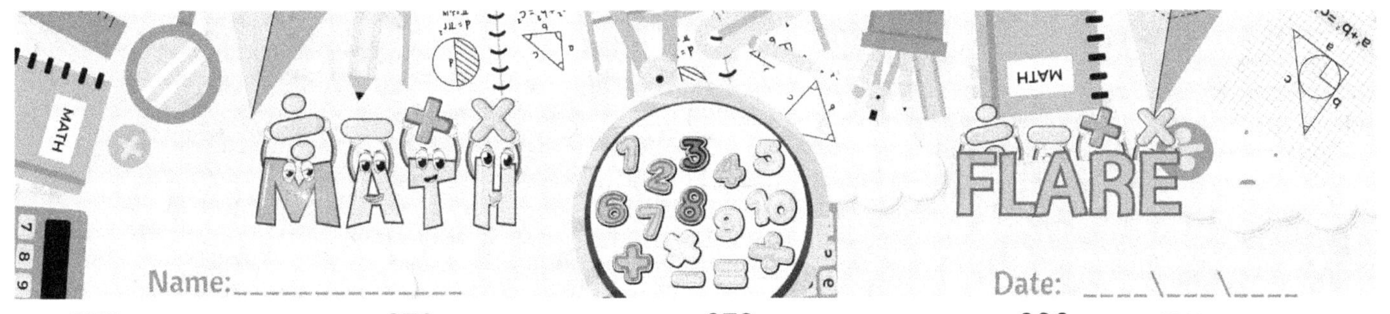

277.	278.	279.	280.
118 - 29	675 - 89	985 - 399	673 - 284

281.	282.	283.	284.
978 - 589	988 - 499	146 - 89	483 - 98

285.	286.	287.	288.
853 - 294	478 - 199	948 - 299	854 - 377

289.	290.	291.	292.
246 - 87	167 - 99	785 - 196	728 - 459

293.	294.	295.	296.
551 - 472	286 - 99	348 - 269	505 - 28

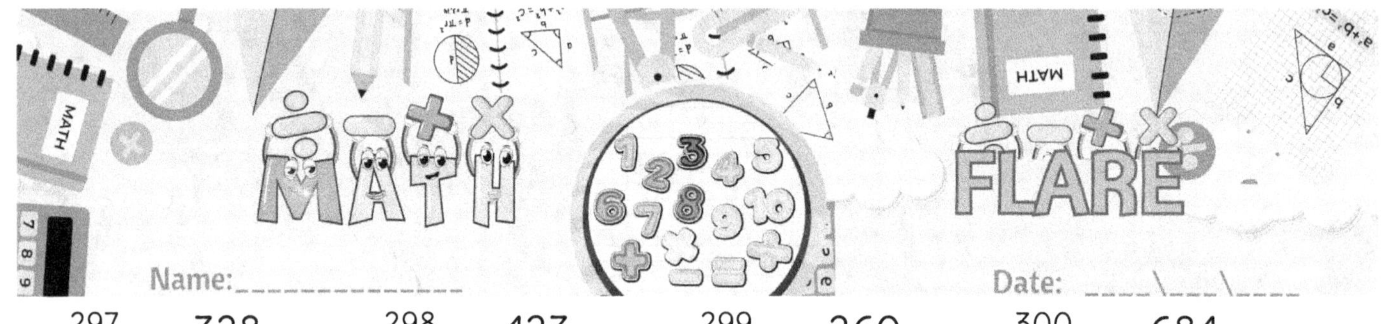

297. 328 − 89	298. 123 − 66	299. 260 − 95	300. 684 − 598
301. 581 − 96	302. 124 − 38	303. 728 − 549	304. 281 − 192
305. 286 − 197	306. 287 − 198	307. 484 − 398	308. 843 − 789
309. 230 − 88	310. 986 − 197	311. 917 − 178	312. 917 − 79
313. 840 − 374	314. 123 − 88	315. 276 − 97	316. 281 − 94

317. 682 – 95	318. 681 – 498	319. 212 – 174	320. 924 – 736
321. 678 – 589	322. 131 – 88	323. 682 – 597	324. 758 – 369
325. 486 – 99	326. 427 – 348	327. 220 – 76	328. 143 – 58
329. 321 – 279	330. 406 – 137	331. 743 – 399	332. 388 – 299
333. 454 – 89	334. 824 – 169	335. 226 – 57	336. 830 – 575

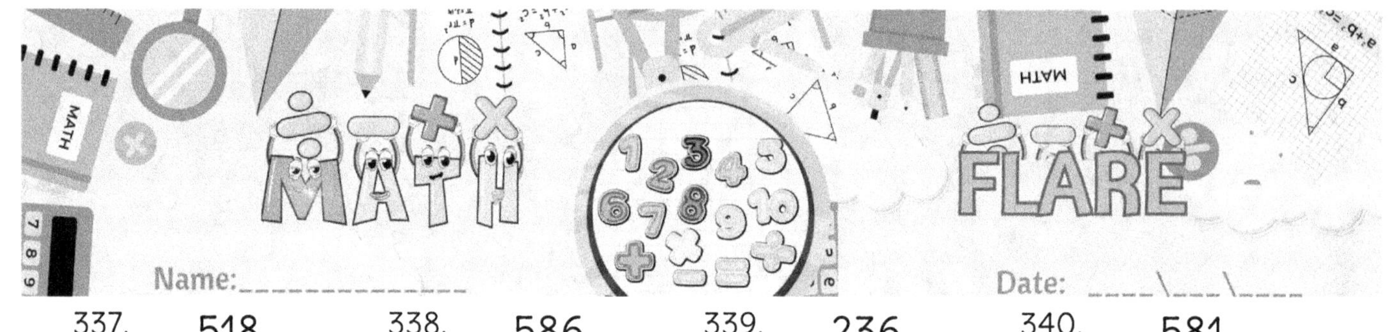

337.	338.	339.	340.
518 - 129	586 - 97	236 - 57	581 - 499

341.	342.	343.	344.
676 - 397	311 - 34	968 - 479	908 - 279

345.	346.	347.	348.
164 - 78	636 - 187	277 - 199	141 - 96

349.	350.	351.	352.
620 - 99	348 - 159	274 - 197	386 - 197

353.	354.	355.	356.
350 - 265	487 - 399	812 - 763	468 - 289

Name:______________________   Date: ____________

357. 716 − 167	358. 371 − 94	359. 917 − 899	360. 348 − 179
361. 213 − 185	362. 548 − 369	363. 570 − 481	364. 271 − 198
365. 676 − 597	366. 966 − 199	367. 668 − 79	368. 304 − 279
369. 845 − 179	370. 177 − 8	371. 561 − 75	372. 268 − 189
373. 782 − 598	374. 914 − 836	375. 824 − 385	376. 324 − 97

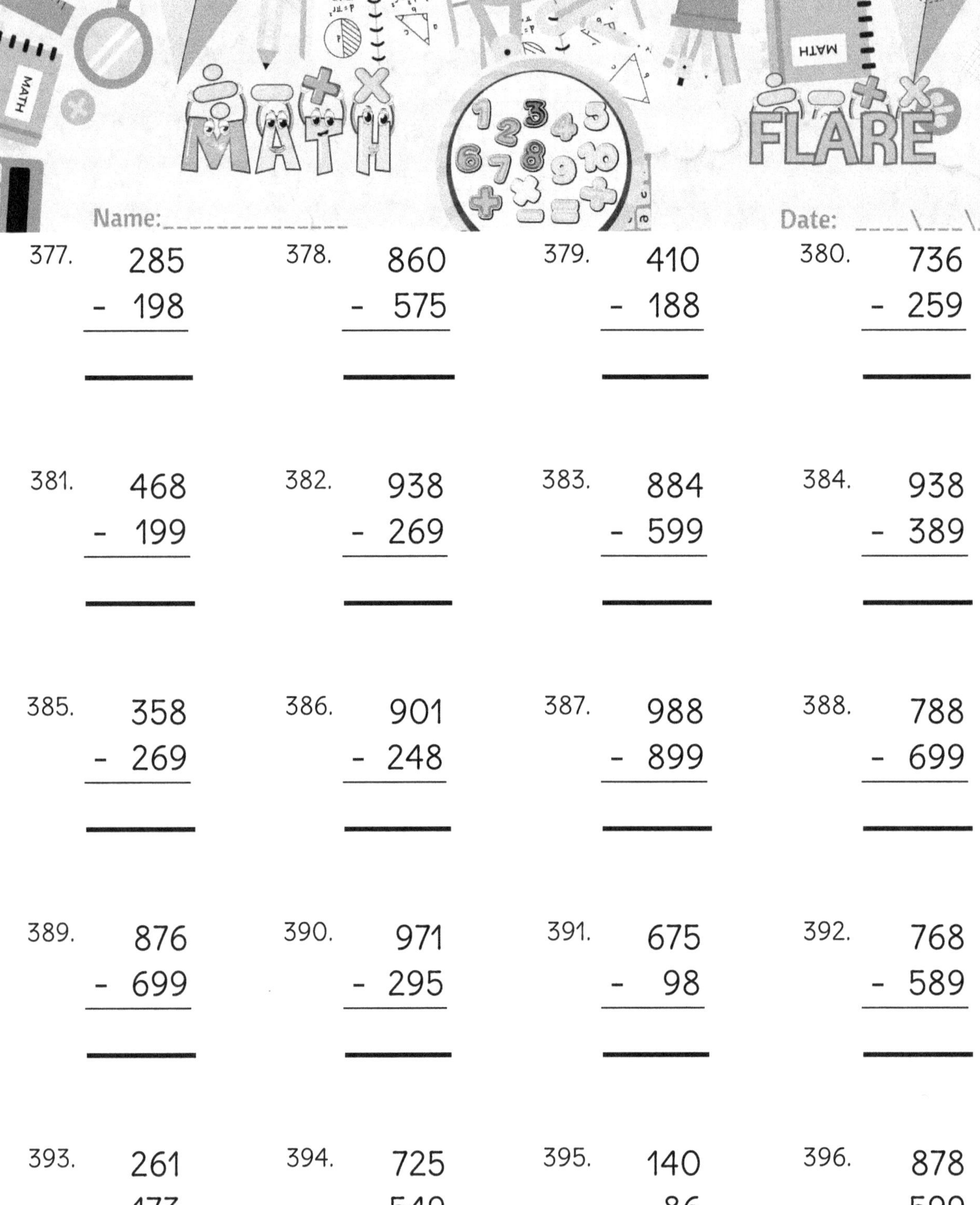

377. 285
  - 198
	378. 860
	  - 575
		379. 410
		  - 188
			380. 736
			  - 259

381. 468
  - 199
	382. 938
	  - 269
		383. 884
		  - 599
			384. 938
			  - 389

385. 358
  - 269
	386. 901
	  - 248
		387. 988
		  - 899
			388. 788
			  - 699

389. 876
  - 699
	390. 971
	  - 295
		391. 675
		  - 98
			392. 768
			  - 589

393. 261
  - 173
	394. 725
	  - 549
		395. 140
		  - 86
			396. 878
			  - 599

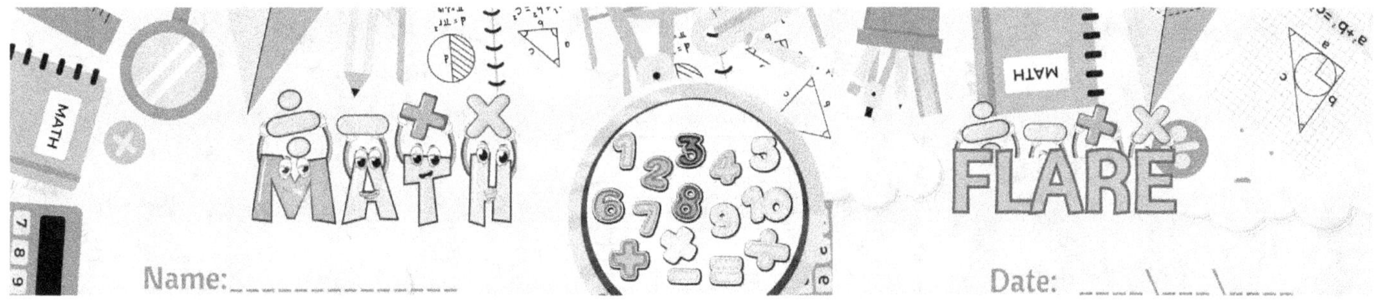

Make 1000

Add a number to the first number to make 100.

397. 83 + ____ = 1,000

398. 73 + ____ = 1,000

399. 10 + ____ = 1,000

400. 32 + ____ = 1,000

401. 72 + ____ = 1,000

402. 60 + ____ = 1,000

403. 90 + ____ = 1,000

404. 52 + ____ = 1,000

405. 28 + ____ = 1,000

406. 70 + ____ = 1,000

407. 87 + ____ = 1,000

408. 86 + ____ = 1,000

409. 68 + ____ = 1,000

410. 76 + ____ = 1,000

411. 11 + ____ = 1,000

412. 57 + ____ = 1,000

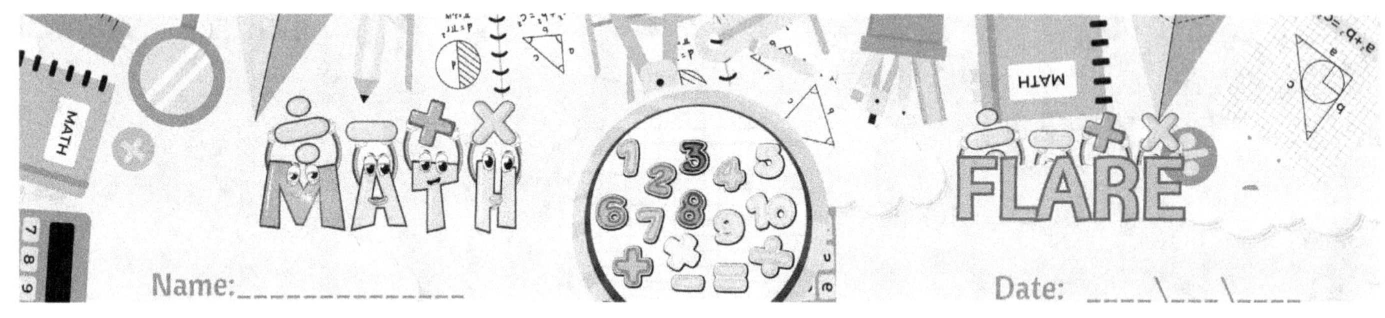

Name:_______________   Date: ____________

413. 75 + _____ = 1,000

414. 5 + _____ = 1,000

415. 67 + _____ = 1,000

416. 51 + _____ = 1,000

417. 35 + _____ = 1,000

418. 9 + _____ = 1,000

419. 43 + _____ = 1,000

420. 15 + _____ = 1,000

421. 64 + _____ = 1,000

422. 13 + _____ = 1,000

423. 17 + _____ = 1,000

424. 27 + _____ = 1,000

425. 66 + _____ = 1,000

426. 38 + _____ = 1,000

427. 80 + _____ = 1,000

428. 49 + _____ = 1,000

429. 23 + _____ = 1,000

430. 55 + _____ = 1,000

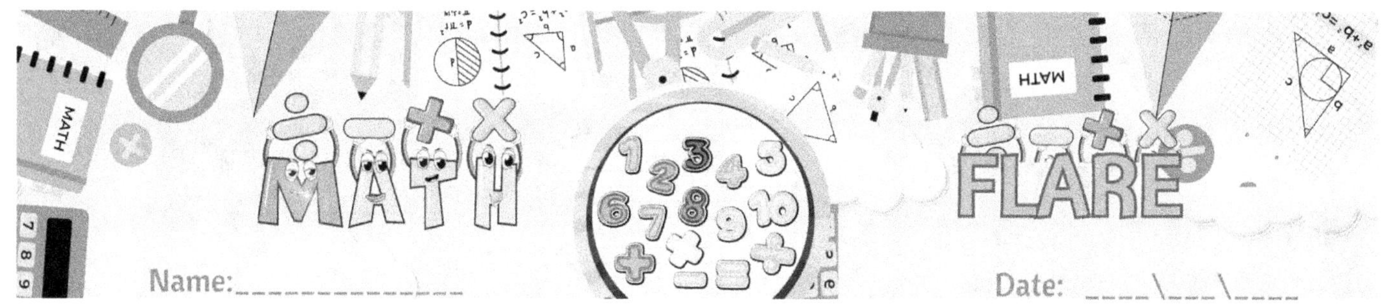

431. 26 + ____ = 1,000

432. 69 + ____ = 1,000

433. 59 + ____ = 1,000

434. 42 + ____ = 1,000

435. 63 + ____ = 1,000

436. 47 + ____ = 1,000

437. 82 + ____ = 1,000

438. 12 + ____ = 1,000

439. 7 + ____ = 1,000

440. 8 + ____ = 1,000

441. 44 + ____ = 1,000

442. 99 + ____ = 1,000

443. 89 + ____ = 1,000

444. 53 + ____ = 1,000

445. 18 + ____ = 1,000

446. 91 + ____ = 1,000

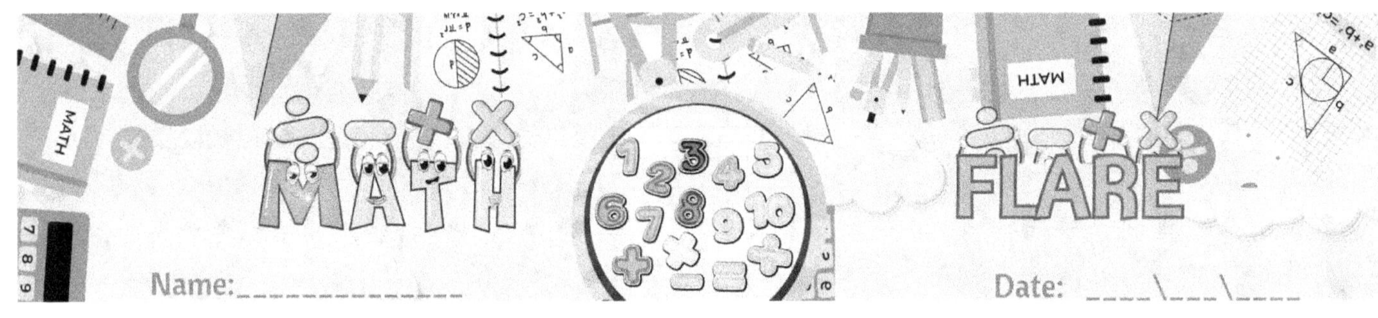

Matching the answers.

447.

a. 942 - 326 = _______ •	• H = 413
b. 108 + 510 = _______ •	• C = 616
c. 347 + 778 = _______ •	• D = 618
d. 783 - 581 = _______ •	• B = 202
e. 700 + 207 = _______ •	• G = 571
f. 257 + 848 = _______ •	• A = 100
g. 765 + 574 = _______ •	• E = 1,125
h. 899 - 328 = _______ •	• F = 1,105
i. 751 - 338 = _______ •	• J = 1,339
j. 322 - 222 = _______ •	• I = 907

Name:________________   Date: _____________

448.

a. 135 + 123 = ______   •   • A = 793

b. 268 + 525 = ______   •   • I = 1,181

c. 350 + 916 = ______   •   • F = 197

d. 110 − 104 = ______   •   • E = 6

e. 655 + 561 = ______   •   • G = 1,216

f. 739 + 559 = ______   •   • C = 1,298

g. 483 + 699 = ______   •   • D = 1,266

h. 961 + 229 = ______   •   • J = 1,182

i. 550 + 631 = ______   •   • H = 258

j. 498 − 301 = ______   •   • B = 1,190

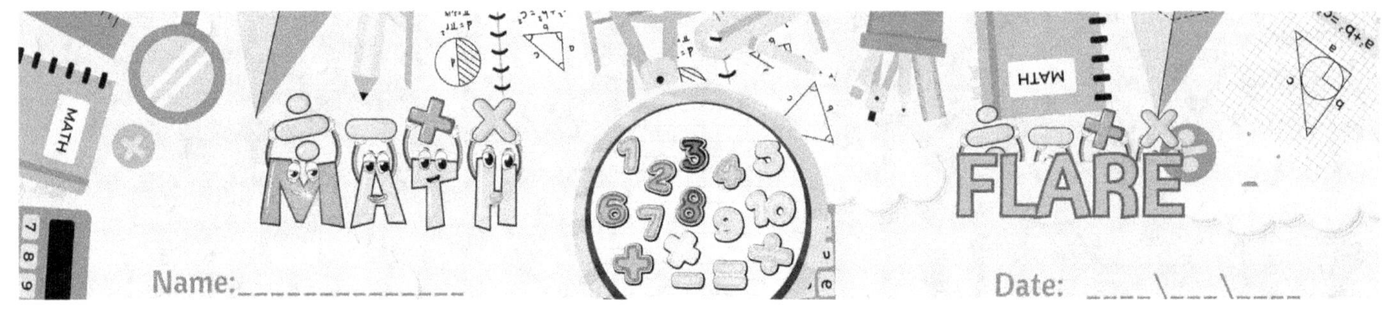

449.

a. 382 + 408 = _______ •   • I = 11

b. 969 - 686 = _______ •   • B = 1,011

c. 789 - 297 = _______ •   • F = 283

d. 726 + 285 = _______ •   • E = 623

e. 848 - 139 = _______ •   • D = 790

f. 163 - 152 = _______ •   • G = 748

g. 565 + 639 = _______ •   • H = 709

h. 149 + 474 = _______ •   • J = 702

i. 403 + 299 = _______ •   • A = 1,204

j. 376 + 372 = _______ •   • C = 492

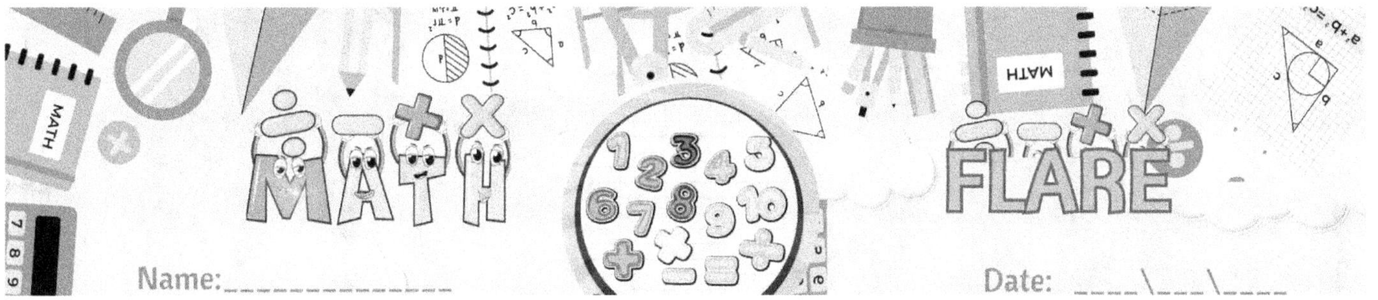

450.

a. 924 + 146 = ______   •   • E = 1,070

b. 721 + 862 = ______   •   • C = 1,289

c. 592 + 532 = ______   •   • G = 1,124

d. 770 + 819 = ______   •   • A = 823

e. 973 + 898 = ______   •   • I = 1,589

f. 380 + 443 = ______   •   • D = 16

g. 567 - 446 = ______   •   • B = 1,871

h. 735 + 554 = ______   •   • H = 563

i. 359 + 204 = ______   •   • F = 121

j. 383 - 367 = ______   •   • J = 1,583

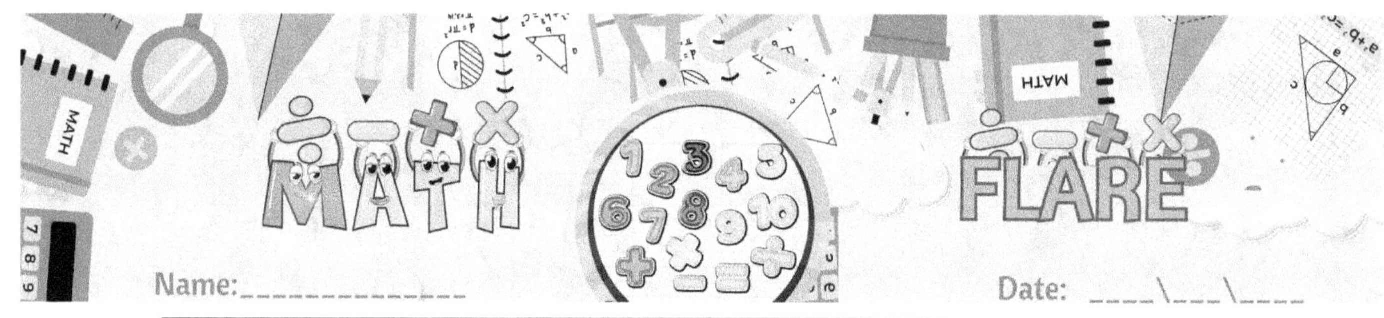

451.

a. 785 - 516 = _______ •   • J = 320

b. 802 + 752 = _______ •   • F = 1,951

c. 964 + 987 = _______ •   • E = 823

d. 619 + 456 = _______ •   • G = 96

e. 820 - 803 = _______ •   • D = 92

f. 576 + 247 = _______ •   • B = 269

g. 856 + 798 = _______ •   • H = 1,554

h. 506 - 410 = _______ •   • C = 17

i. 569 - 249 = _______ •   • A = 1,654

j. 502 - 410 = _______ •   • I = 1,075

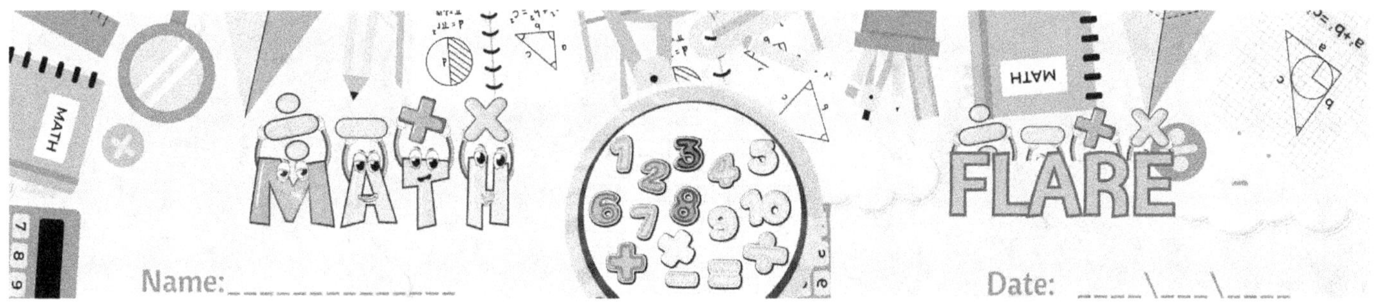

Name:_______________   Date: _____________

452.

a. 126 − 115 = _______ •	• E = 1,032
b. 470 + 726 = _______ •	• C = 1,183
c. 922 + 261 = _______ •	• I = 970
d. 938 − 837 = _______ •	• B = 11
e. 830 + 140 = _______ •	• D = 251
f. 842 + 136 = _______ •	• H = 108
g. 470 − 219 = _______ •	• F = 978
h. 444 + 420 = _______ •	• G = 864
i. 230 − 122 = _______ •	• J = 1,196
j. 304 + 728 = _______ •	• A = 101

MathFlare - Addition and Subtraction 2nd and 3rd Grade

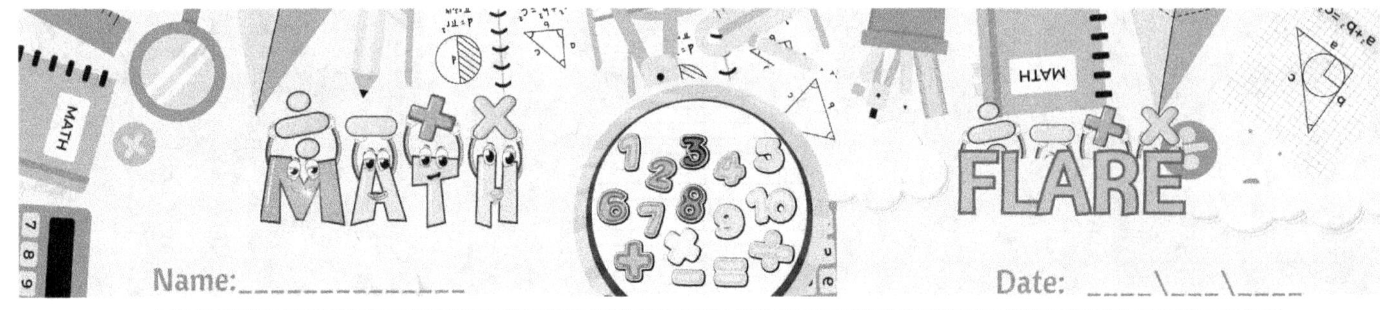

453.

a. 670 + 997 = _______ •	• E = 1,612
b. 596 - 458 = _______ •	• F = 588
c. 899 + 713 = _______ •	• D = 301
d. 918 + 979 = _______ •	• B = 138
e. 743 - 597 = _______ •	• A = 1,667
f. 495 - 194 = _______ •	• H = 1,897
g. 752 - 695 = _______ •	• C = 968
h. 462 + 506 = _______ •	• J = 146
i. 827 - 388 = _______ •	• I = 57
j. 898 - 310 = _______ •	• G = 439

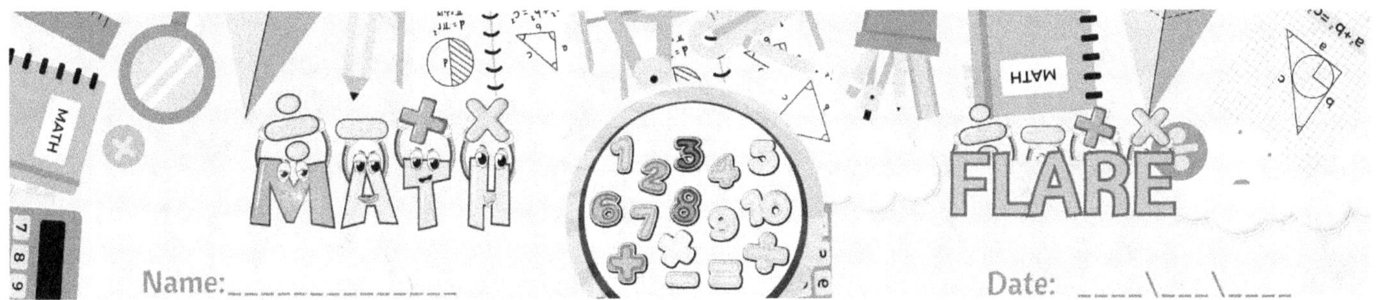

454.

a. 353 + 894 = _______ •	• G = 157
b. 873 + 710 = _______ •	• J = 14
c. 674 + 388 = _______ •	• D = 448
d. 663 – 215 = _______ •	• H = 11
e. 224 – 210 = _______ •	• C = 354
f. 390 – 233 = _______ •	• B = 167
g. 338 – 171 = _______ •	• I = 1,062
h. 234 + 120 = _______ •	• A = 36
i. 202 – 191 = _______ •	• F = 1,583
j. 236 – 200 = _______ •	• E = 1,247

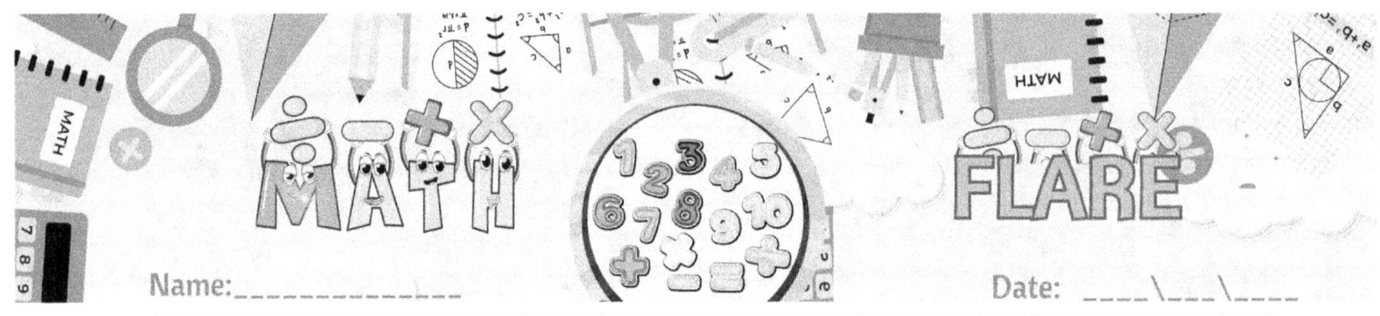

Name:________________   Date: ___________

a. 962 - 945 = _______ •	• B = 662
b. 576 + 336 = _______ •	• G = 17
c. 316 + 627 = _______ •	• F = 752
d. 787 + 217 = _______ •	• D = 933
e. 395 + 357 = _______ •	• A = 816
f. 227 - 184 = _______ •	• H = 43
g. 272 + 661 = _______ •	• C = 1,004
h. 118 + 334 = _______ •	• E = 452
i. 517 + 299 = _______ •	• J = 943
j. 524 + 138 = _______ •	• I = 912

456.

a. 597 + 471 = _______   •   • B = 1,505

b. 531 + 989 = _______   •   • G = 13

c. 105 - 101 = _______   •   • C = 387

d. 568 - 555 = _______   •   • F = 4

e. 913 + 592 = _______   •   • H = 1,207

f. 773 - 769 = _______   •   • J = 1,068

g. 990 + 217 = _______   •   • I = 26

h. 138 - 112 = _______   •   • E = 4

i. 393 - 262 = _______   •   • A = 131

j. 837 - 450 = _______   •   • D = 1,520

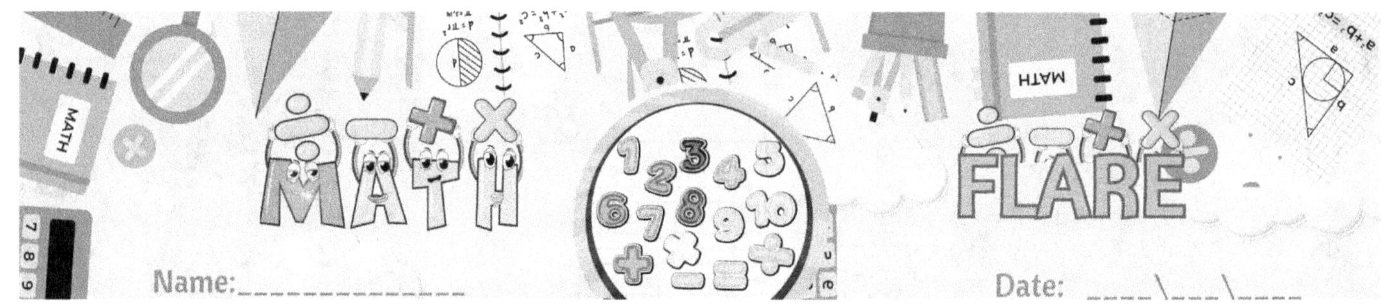

Addition Word Problems

457. At the beginning of the week, there were 18 apples in the basket. By the end of the week, 4 more apples were added to the basket. How many apples are in the basket now?

458. A bakery sold 4 cupcakes in the morning and 17 cupcakes in the afternoon. How many cupcakes did the bakery sell in total?

459. Zachary had 17 dollars in the morning and earned 10 more dollars in the afternoon. How many dollars Zachary have in total?

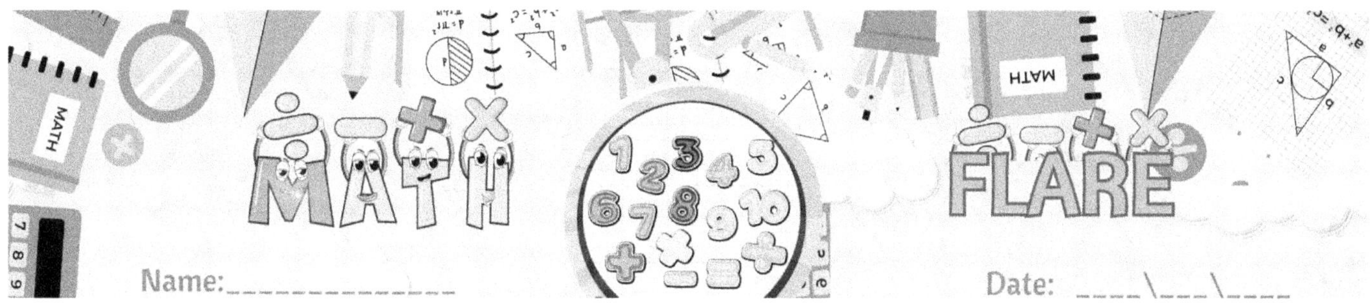

460. There are 4 trees in the garden. 11 more trees are planted. How many trees are in the garden now?

461. On Monday, Bella solved 14 math problems, and on Tuesday, Bella solved 6 problems. How many math problems did Bella solve?

462. At the start of the school year, there were 10 students enrolled in English class. By the end of the year, 17 more students had enrolled. How many students were enrolled in English class at the end of the year?

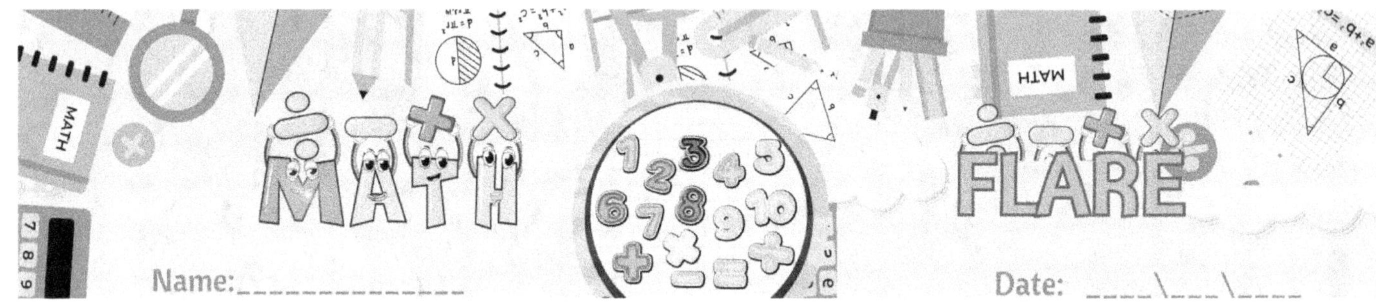

463. A bus made 18 stops in the morning and 8 stops in the afternoon. How many stops did the bus make in total?

464. There is 1 ointment on the shelf. Ariana puts 17 more ointments on the shelf. How many ointments are there on the shelf now?

465. At the store, Wesley bought 12 pianos. Later, Hannah bought 19 pianos from the same store. How many pianos were bought in total?

466. Yesterday, Camila earned $5, and today, Camila earned $13. How much money did Camila earn in total?

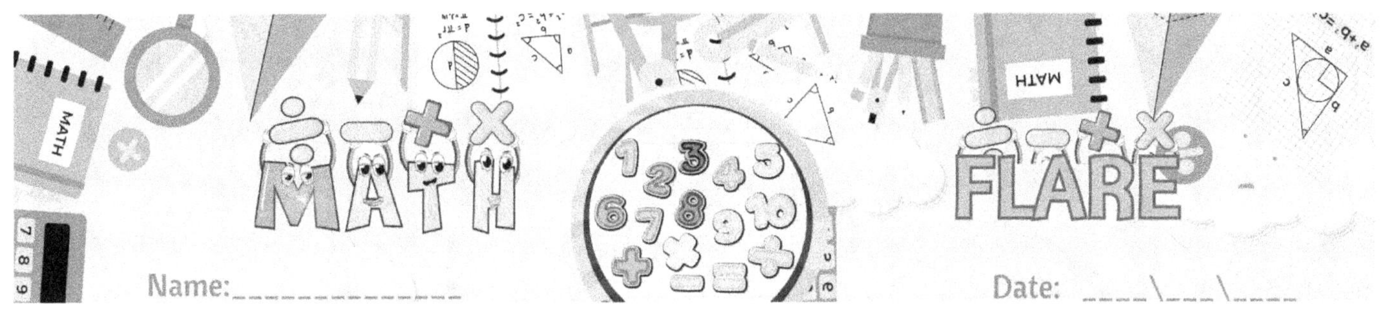

467. On Monday, Lincoln did 15 math problems. On Tuesday, Lincoln did 15 more math problems. How many math problems did Lincoln do in total?

468. Liam had 5 dollars and earned 7 more dollars. How much money does Liam have now?

469. A basketball team scored 20 points in the first quarter and 13 points in the second quarter. What was the total score of the basketball team after the first half?

470. Evan has 16 muffins. He receives 4 more muffins. How many muffins does he have now?

Name:_________________

Date: ______________

471. A basket holds 9 thermometers. If 9 more thermometers are added to the basket, how many thermometers will the basket hold in total?

472. Andrew has 3 apples and 3 oranges in a basket. How many fruits does Andrew have in total?

473. Adalyn sold 6 cups on Monday and 5 cups on Tuesday. How many cups did the she sell in total?

474. Bella watched 6 movies last week and 5 movies this week. How many movies did Bella watch altogether?

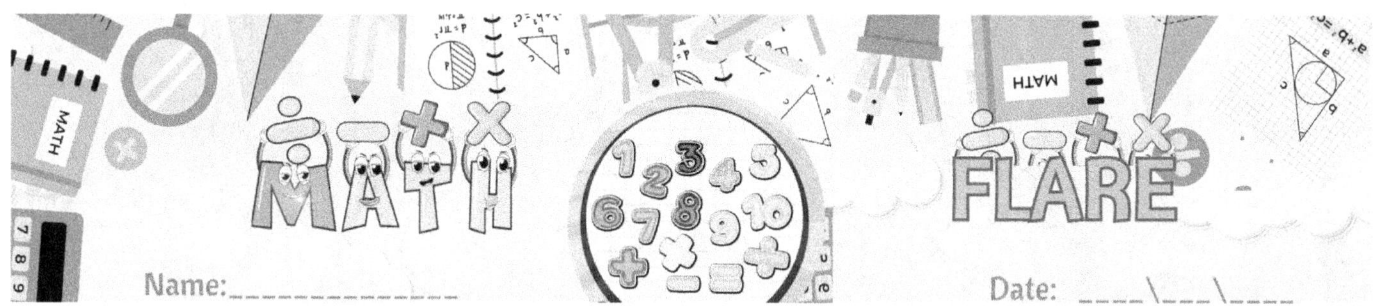

475. On Monday, Addison caught 9 fish, and on Tuesday, Addison caught 12 fish. How many fish did Addison catch in total?

476. There are 19 apples in the bag. If 14 more apples are added, how many apples are in the bag now?

477. Benjamin made 16 cookies and Hailey made 18 cookies. How many cookies were made in total?

478. At the beginning of the week, there were 3 scarves in the bag. By the end of the week, 8 more scarves were added to the bag. How many scarves are in the bag now?

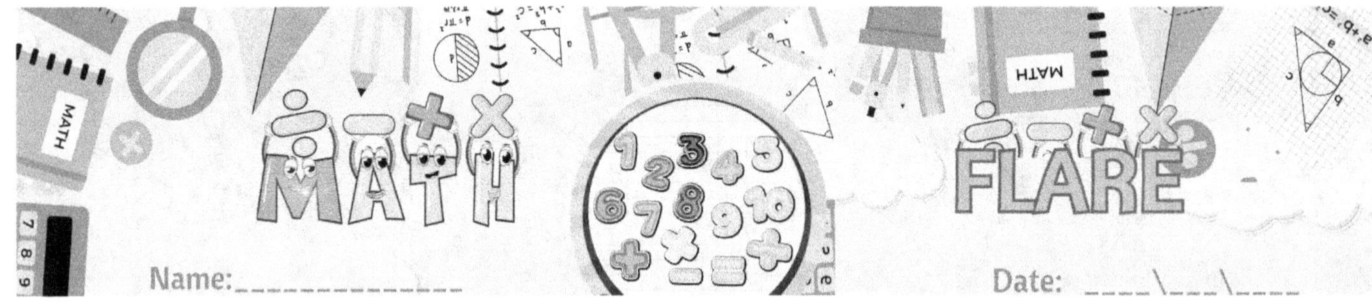

479. Micah has 12 dollars and found 17 more dollars on the ground. How much money does Micah have now?

480. Everly walked 16 miles yesterday and 3 miles today. How many miles did Everly walk in total?

481. Ian bought 7 pencils and 16 pens. How many writing instruments did Ian buy in total?

482. Diego has 7 pencils and 2 pens. If Diego puts all the writing utensils in a case, how many writing utensils are in the case in total?

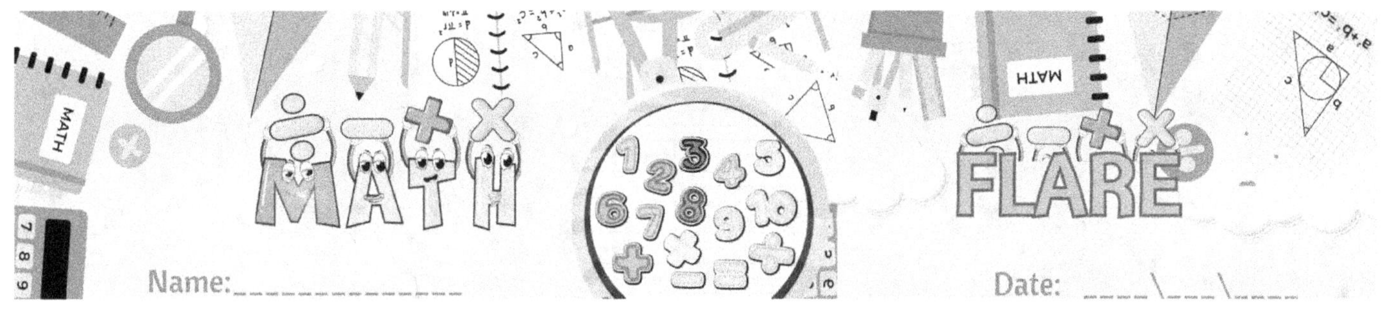

483. Ella baked 4 cakes yesterday and 5 cakes today. How many cakes did Ella bake in total?

484. Thomas filled a tank with 7 gallons of gas and then added 4 more gallons. How many gallons of gas are in the tank now?

485. On Monday, Nova read 20 pages, and on Tuesday, 18 pages. How many pages did Nova read altogether?

486. Serenity bought pizzas with 18 slices. Later, Serenity bought some more pizzas with 5 slices. How many slices of pizzas does Serenity have in total?

Subtraction Word Problems

487. Aaron has 15 bags. He traded 11 of them with his friend. How many bags does Aaron have now?

488. A pack of gum had 19 pieces. Emily took 19 pieces of gum. How many pieces of gum are left in the pack?

489. Pencils originally cost 10 dollars, but it is now on sale for 7 dollars. How much money can you save by buying it on sale?

490. Jayden saved up 6 dollars to buy calendars. He spent 1 dollars on it. How much money does he have left?

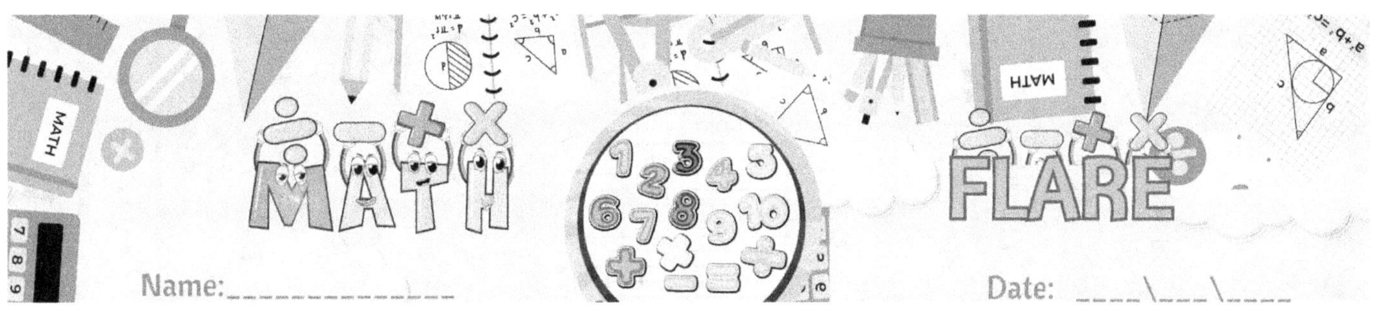

491. There are 2 fish in a tank. If 1 leave, how many fish are left in the tank?

492. Emma bought books for 19 dollars but later found out it was on sale for 14 dollars less. How much did she overpay for books?

493. There are 17 cars in a parking lot. Ethan took 1 cars out of the lot. How many cars are still in the lot?

494. Layla and Hazel went shopping for rulers. They had 14 dollars to spend but 3 dollars ended up being spent. How much money do they have left?

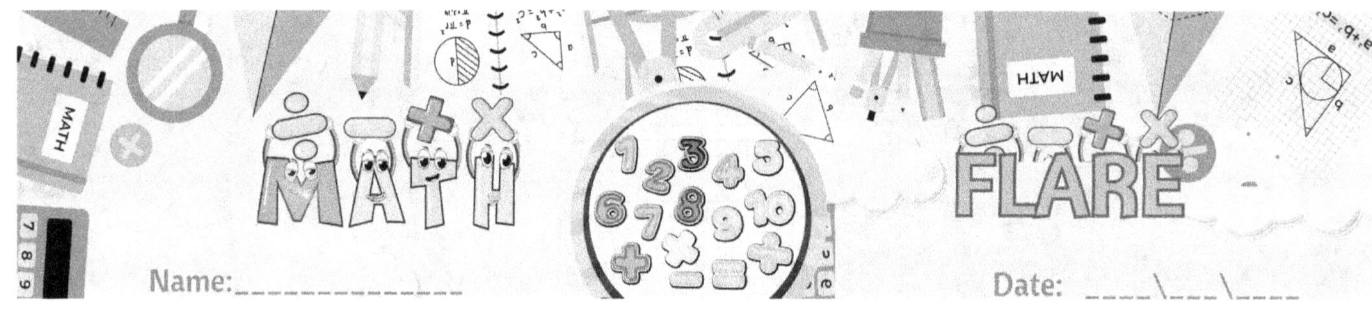

495. There are 8 fish in a pond. Harper caught 2 fish. How many fish are left in the pond?

496. If you have 19 needles and you give away 4, how many needles do you have left?

497. A folders costs $7 and a pen costs $1. How much more expensive is the folders than the pen?

498. Aria bought perfumes for 16 dollars. She later returned some perfumes and received a refund of 14 dollars. How much money did she end up spending on perfumes?

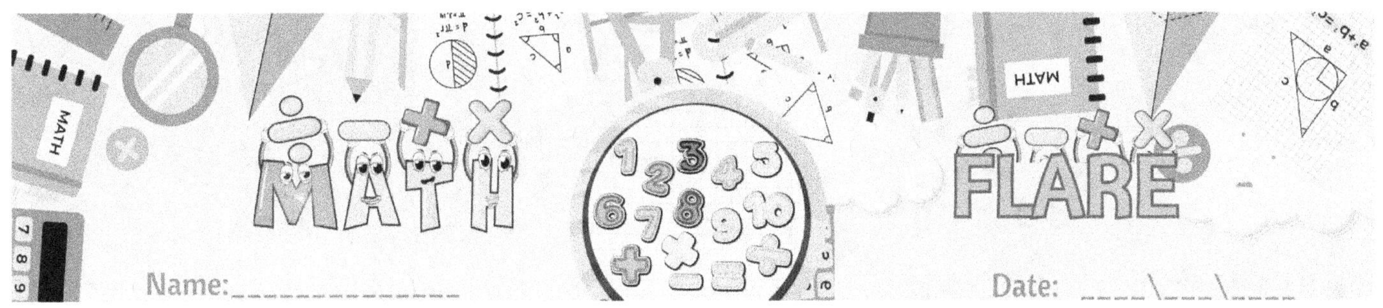

499. Adam has 1 dollars. He needs to buy tissues that costs 2 dollars. How much money will he have left after buying the tissues?

500. Aiden had 10 bagels. He gave 3 bagels to Alexa. How many bagels does Aiden have left?

501. There are 6 turtles in a pond. If 2 leave, how many turtles are left in the pond?

502. Kingston is 8 years old and Josiah is 4 years old. What is the difference in their ages?

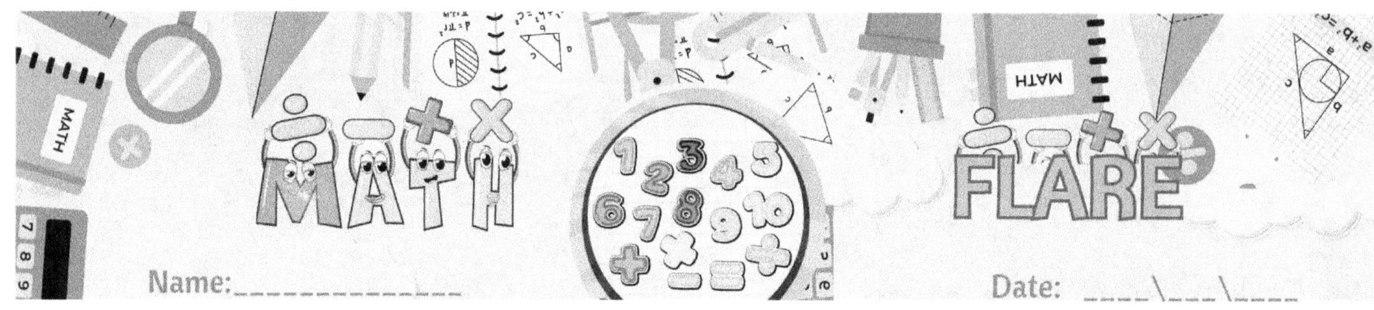

503. Maria has 6 dollars. She wants to buy flosses, which costs 20 dollars. How much more money does she need to buy it?

504. Clocks costs 19 dollars. If you paid $5. How much change will you get back?

505. If globes costs 16 dollars and you have 13 dollars, how much more money do you need to buy it?

506. A pizza has 12 slices. Genesis ate 10 slices. How many slices of pizza are left?

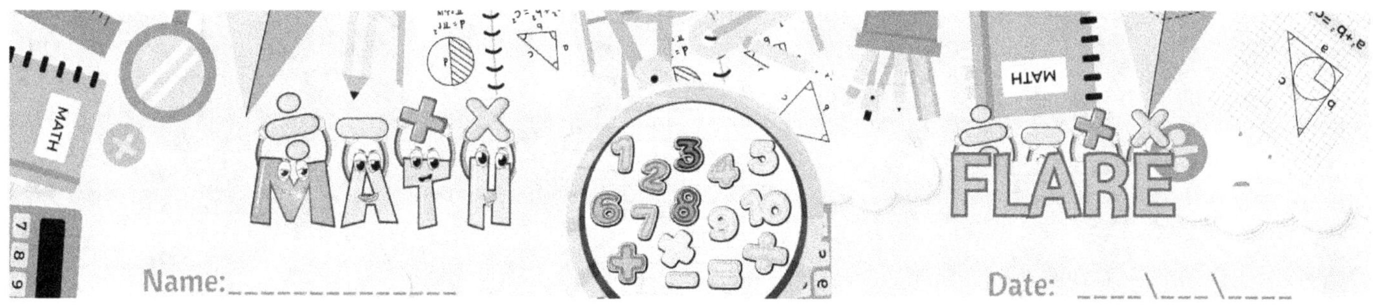

507. Ryan had 16 dollars. He spent 8 dollars on a thermometers. How much money does Ryan have left?

508. There are 10 dogs in a park. If 1 leave, how many dogs are left in the park?

509. Luna bought violins for 19 dollars. She received 16 dollars in change. How much did violins cost?

510. Madelyn has 6 rocks in her collection. She gave 2 of them to her friend. How many rocks does Madelyn have now?

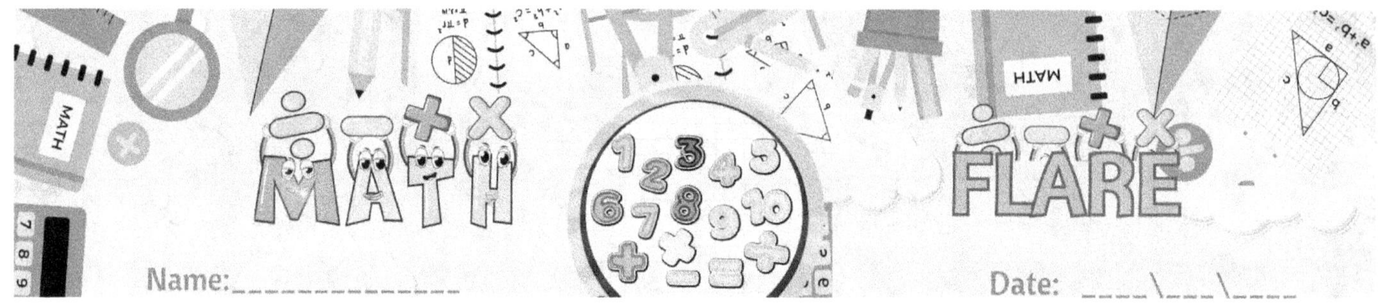

511. Kinsley wants to buy vitamins, which costs 5 dollars. She has 2 dollars and plans to save the rest. How much more money does she need to save to buy vitamins?

512. Lucas has 16 dollars. He wants to buy bandages that costs 2 dollars. How much more money does he need to buy the bandages?

513. Genesis has 20 shirts. She lost 10 of them. How many shirts does Genesis have left?

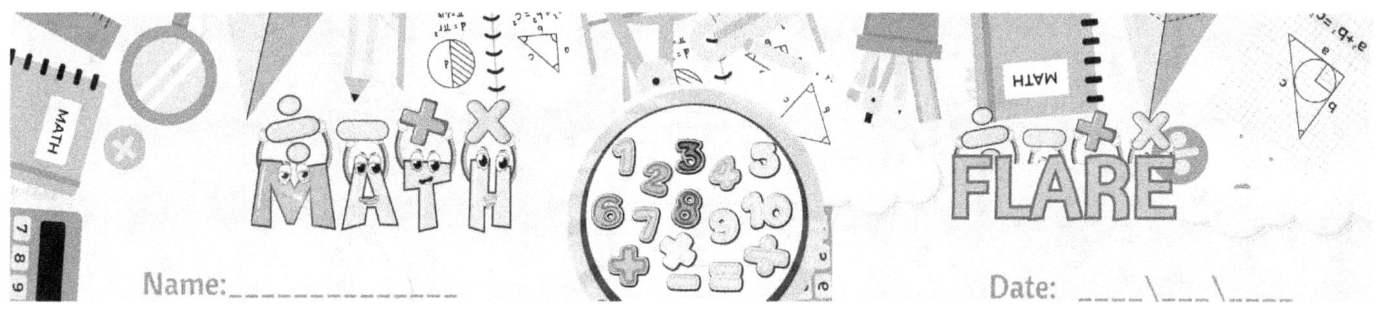

514. Paisley baked a 15 cookies. 5 of them were chocolate chip cookies and the rest were oatmeal raisin cookies. How many oatmeal raisin cookies did Paisley bake?

515. Ellie and Riley went on a shopping spree and bought 18 gloves. After returning home, they realized that they didn't need 15 of them. How many gloves did they end up keeping?

516. A recipe needs 17 cups of sugar. Avery added 6 cups of sugar. How many cups of sugar are still needed?

517. There were 2 students in a class. 2 of them were absent. How many students were present in the class?

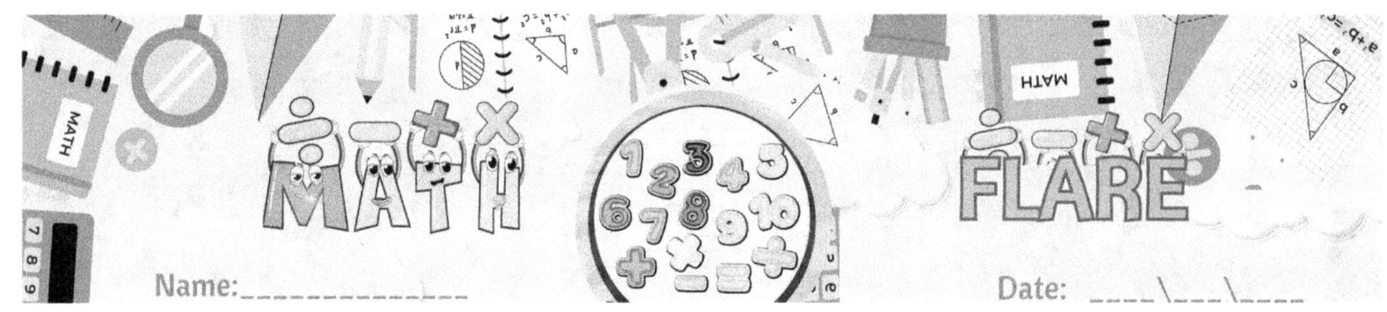

Name:_________________   Date: ____________

Addition Circles

Add.

519.

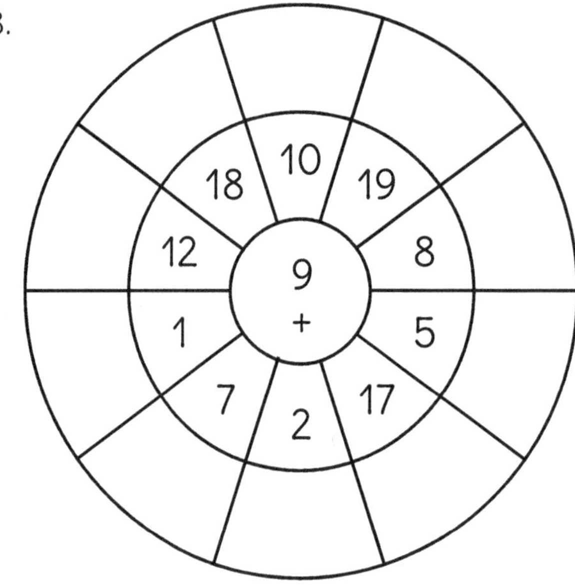

519.

520.

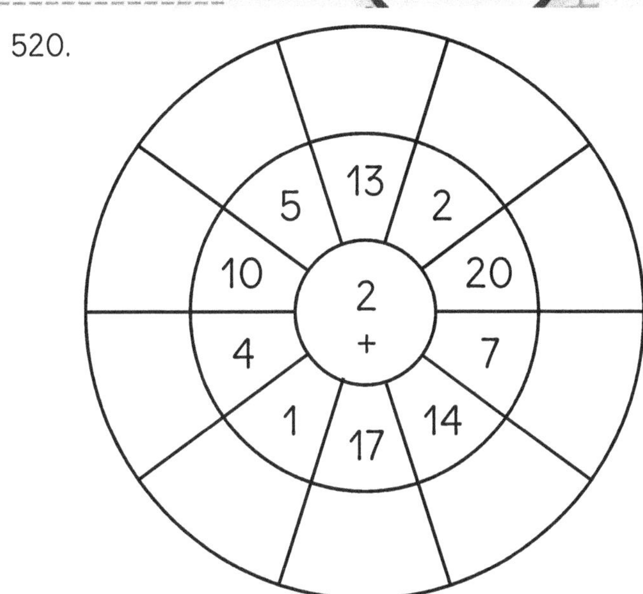

521.

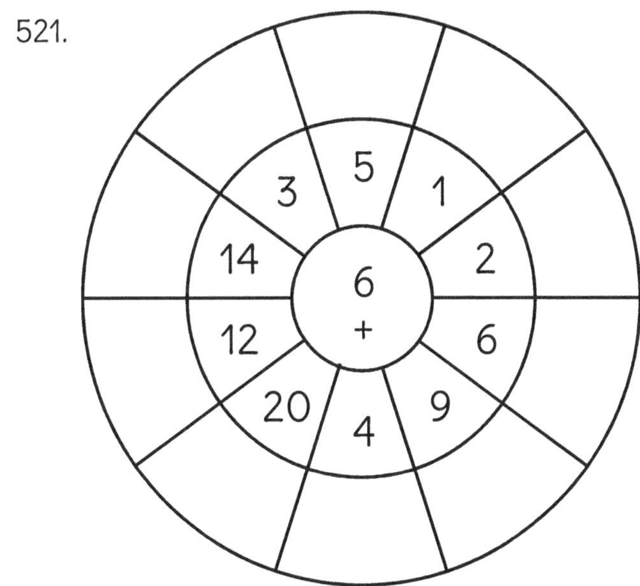

522.

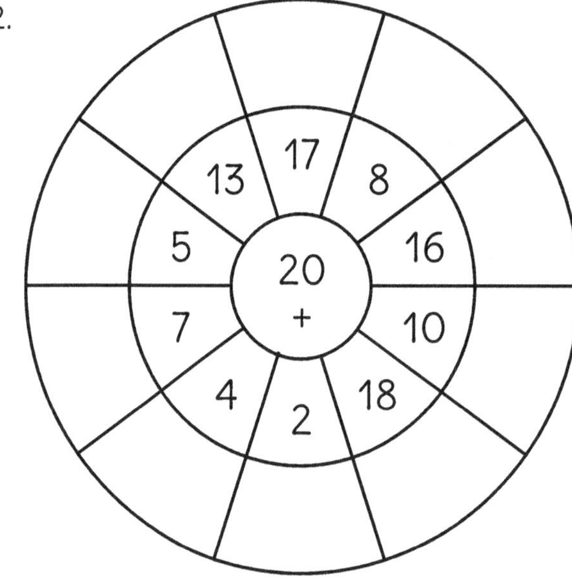

523.

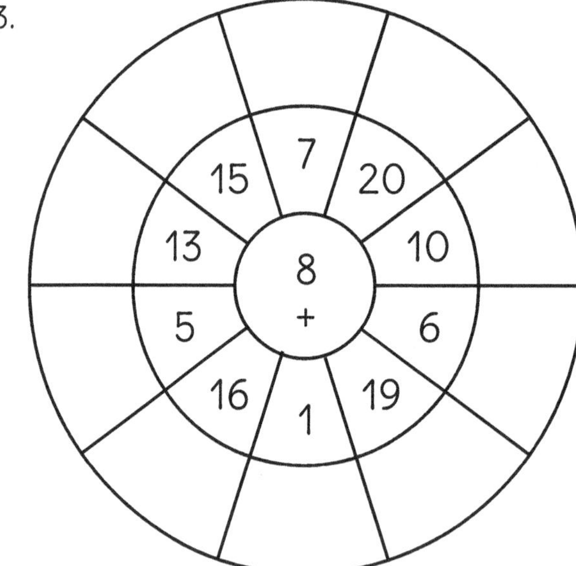

MATH
FLARE
Name:
Date:

13
17
8
5
16
20
+
7
10
4
2
18

15
7
20
13
10
8
+
5
6
16
1
19

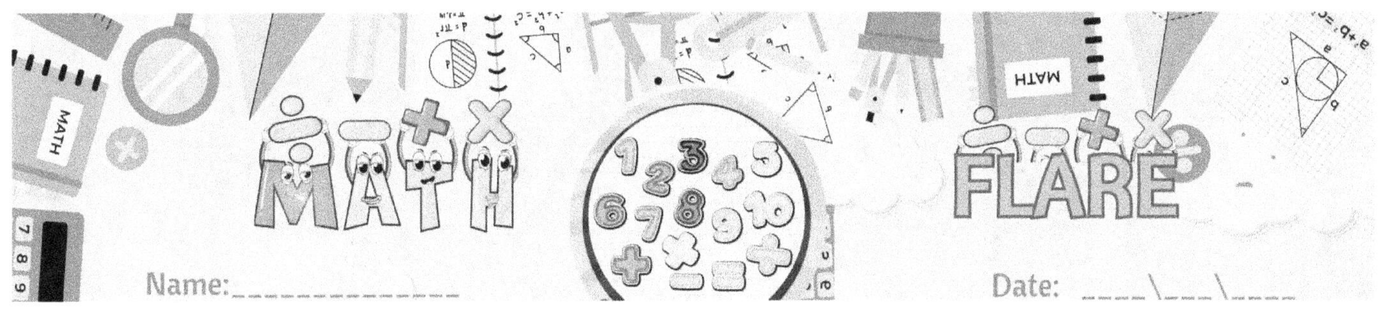

524.

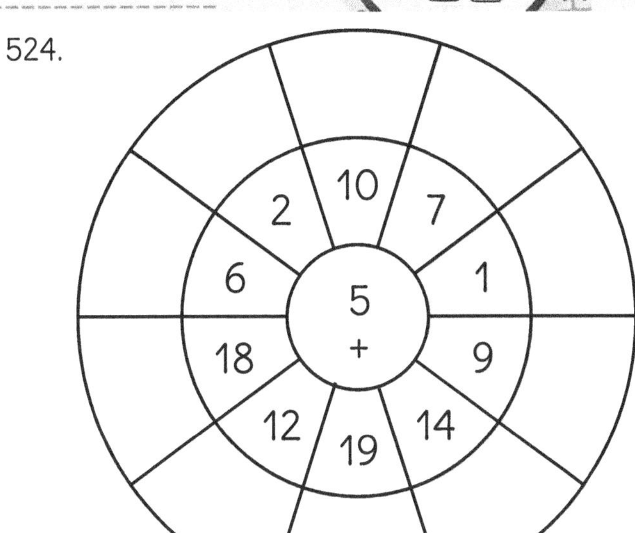

525.

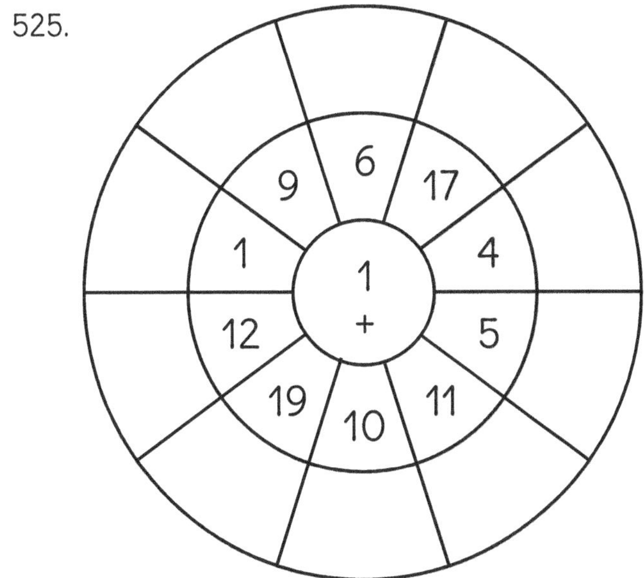

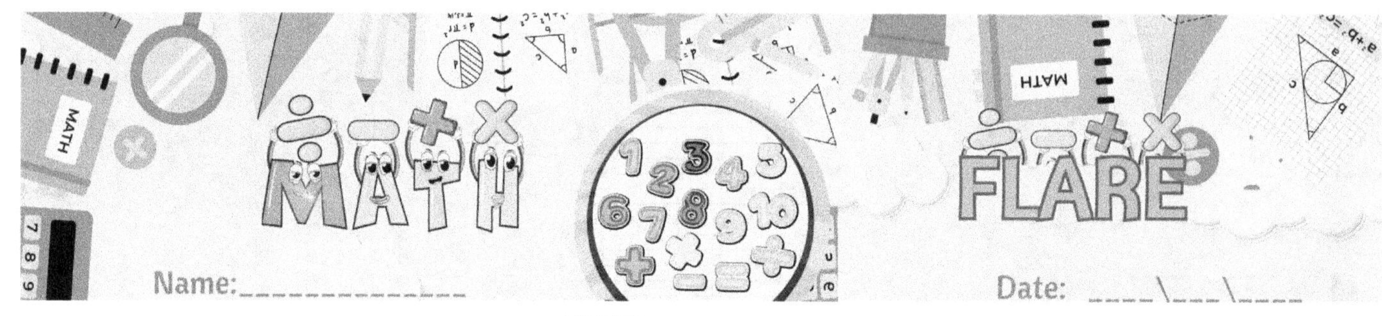

526.

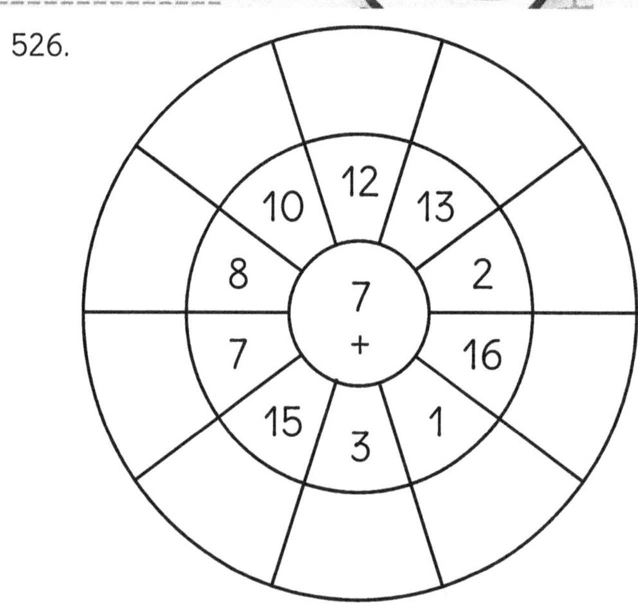

527.

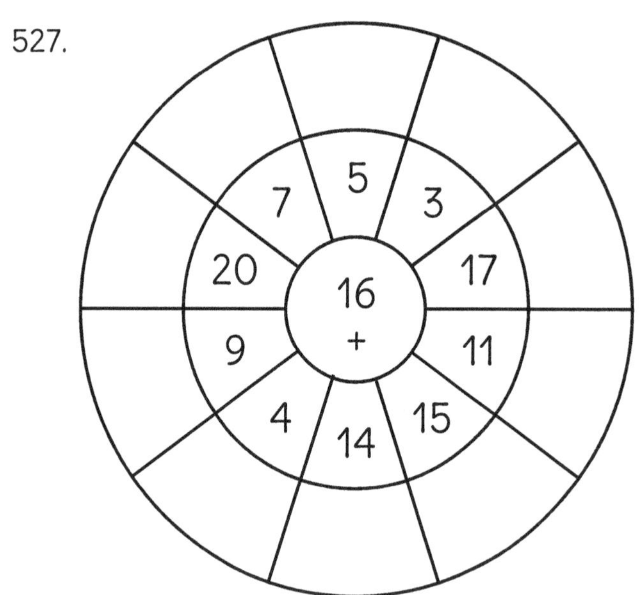

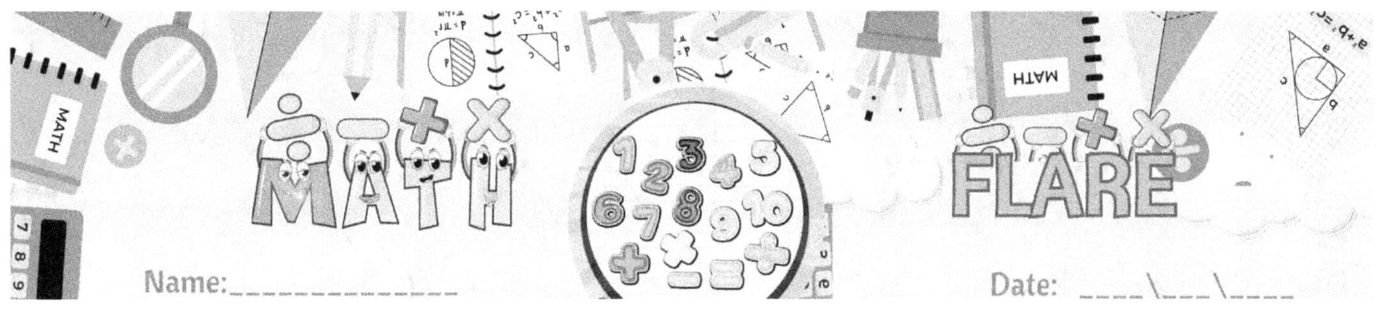

Circle Drills Subtraction

Subtract.

528.

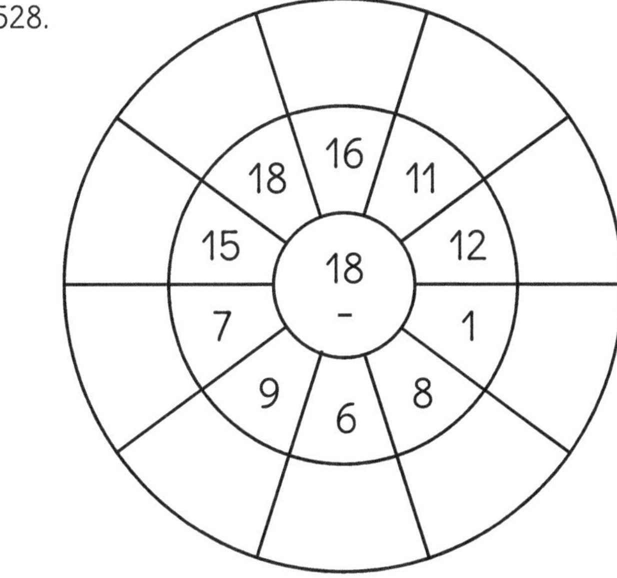

529.

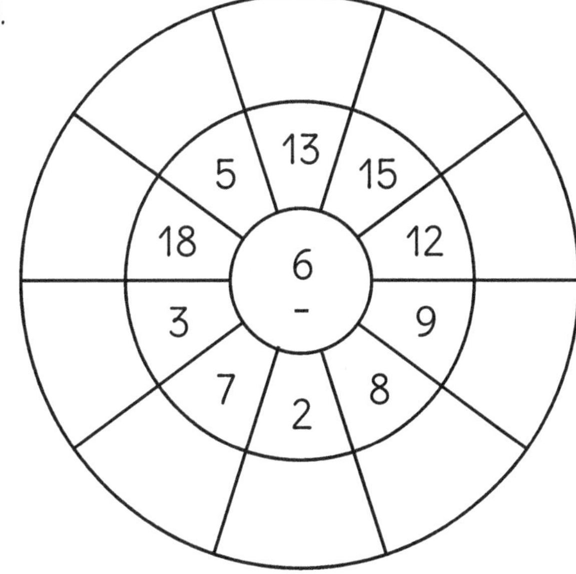

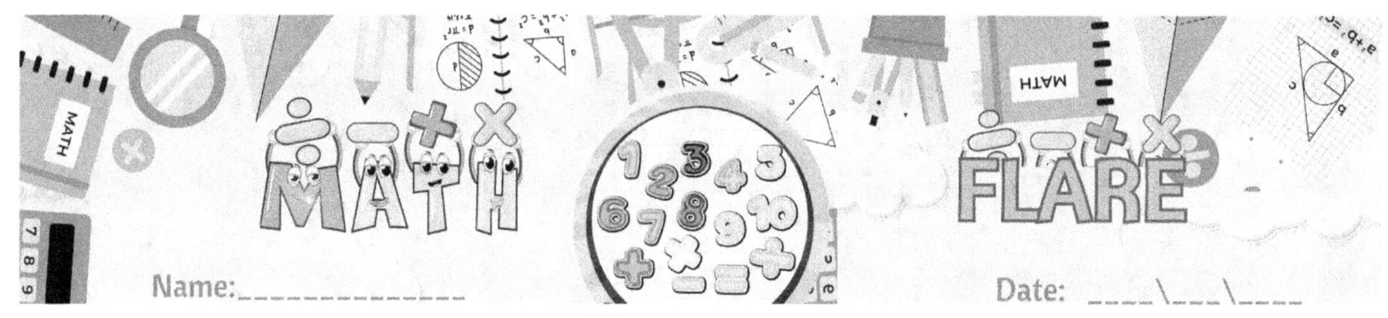

530.

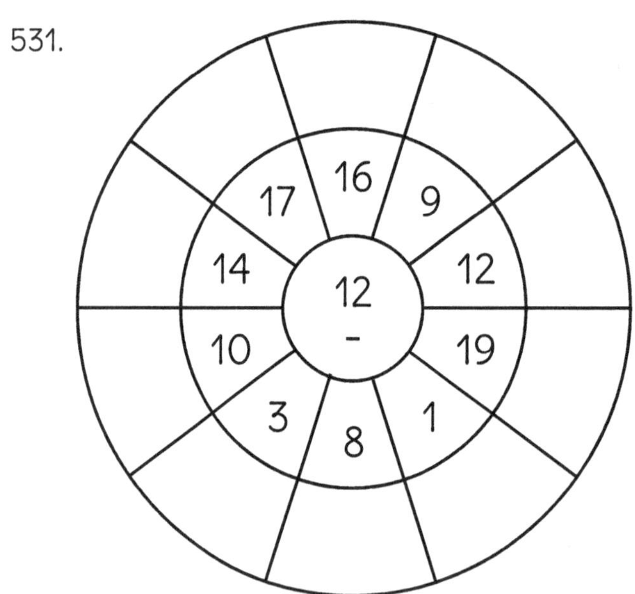

531.

532.

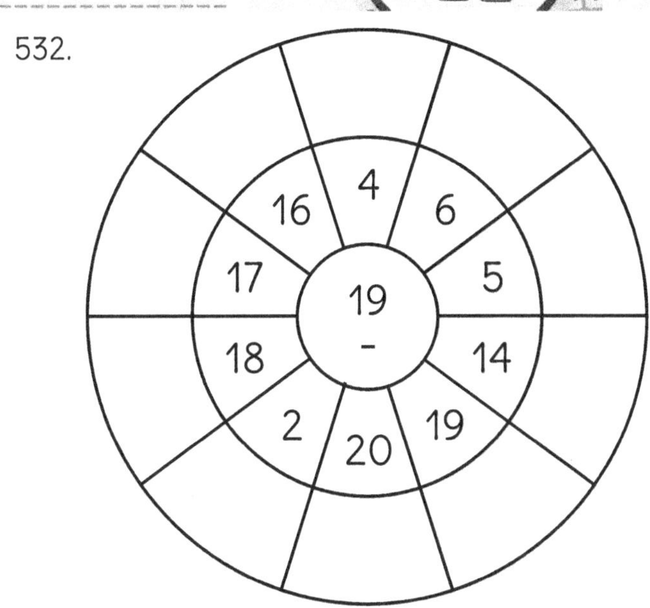

533.

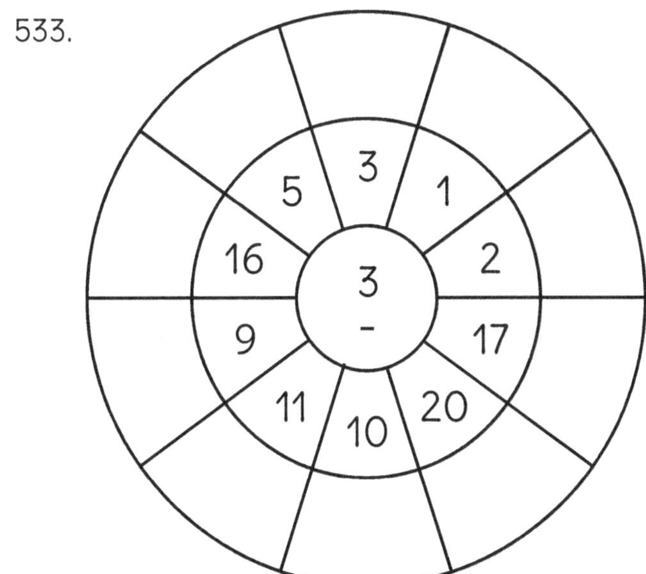

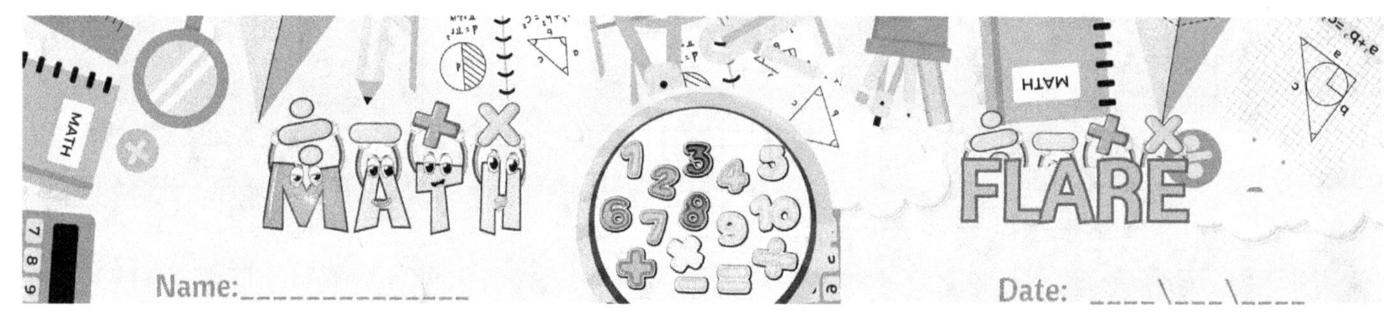

MATH
FLARE
Name:_______________
Date: _____________

13
8
17
2
7
1
-
5
18
19
12
10

16
6
18
3
5
11
-
12
4
13
10
2

534.

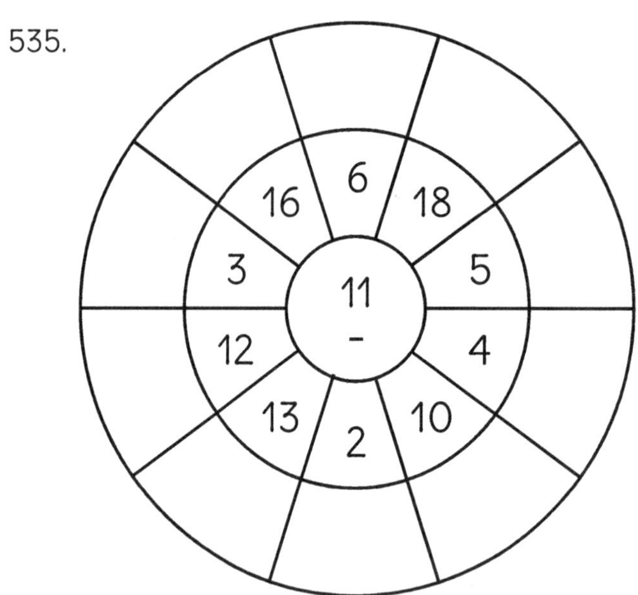

535.

536.

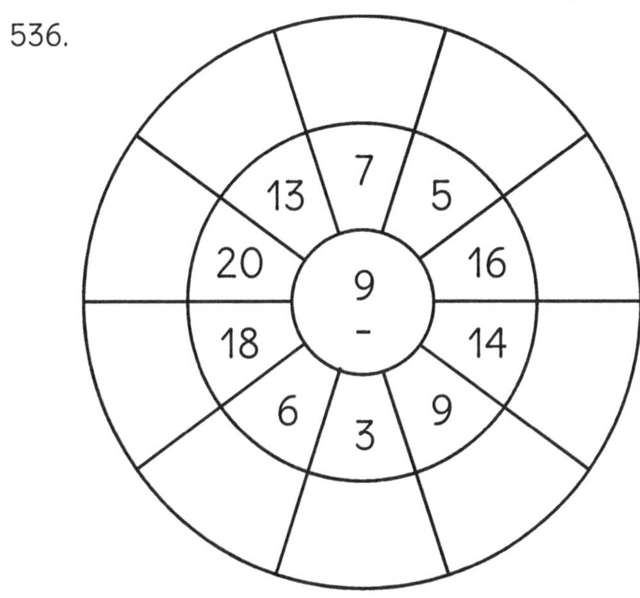

537.

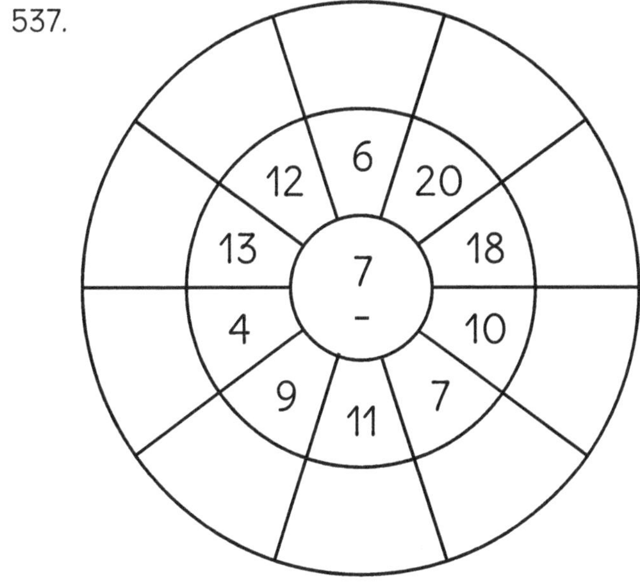

ANSWERS

Page 1: Addition with Regrouping

1. 1,422	2. 1,210	3. 1,114	4. 1,223	5. 1,455
6. 1,210	7. 720	8. 1,145	9. 724	10. 1,211
11. 1,215	12. 1,110	13. 1,116	14. 1,335	15. 1,544
16. 1,544	17. 1,420	18. 1,141	19. 1,470	20. 1,240
21. 1,716	22. 1,132	23. 1,741	24. 1,363	25. 336
26. 1,133	27. 1,232	28. 1,211	29. 1,112	30. 1,044
31. 1,010	32. 1,331	33. 1,313	34. 1,410	35. 1,230
36. 1,110	37. 1,153	38. 241	39. 1,555	40. 1,252
41. 1,783	42. 1,181	43. 1,370	44. 1,241	45. 1,320
46. 1,120	47. 1,533	48. 1,131	49. 1,822	50. 1,110
51. 1,120	52. 1,157	53. 1,220	54. 1,110	55. 1,427
56. 1,110	57. 1,110	58. 950	59. 1,160	60. 310
61. 1,325	62. 1,230	63. 1,631	64. 1,112	65. 1,122
66. 1,610	67. 1,151	68. 1,180	69. 423	70. 1,113
71. 1,111	72. 1,631	73. 1,113	74. 1,113	75. 150
76. 1,230	77. 1,041	78. 1,161	79. 1,332	80. 1,344
81. 1,210	82. 1,216	83. 1,346	84. 1,370	85. 622
86. 1,540	87. 1,240	88. 1,121	89. 1,221	90. 1,122
91. 1,210	92. 1,110	93. 1,617	94. 1,615	95. 1,241

96. 1,623   97. 1,115   98. 411   99. 1,010   100. 1,470

101. 1,235   102. 1,310   103. 1,321   104. 1,221   105. 1,410

106. 1,321   107. 933   108. 1,112   109. 1,730   110. 1,120

111. 413   112. 1,814   113. 1,552   114. 281   115. 1,210

116. 631   117. 1,120   118. 1,615   119. 1,230   120. 244

121. 1,262   122. 1,113   123. 1,016   124. 1,561   125. 1,410

126. 1,123   127. 1,521   128. 1,231   129. 1,210   130. 1,320

131. 1,134   132. 831   133. 1,760   134. 1,140   135. 1,920

136. 1,811   137. 1,613   138. 1,331   139. 1,121   140. 1,760

141. 1,171   142. 1,530   143. 950   144. 1,210   145. 1,421

146. 1,131   147. 441   148. 1,532   149. 1,811   150. 510

151. 1,460   152. 1,220   153. 1,735   154. 1,770   155. 1,172

156. 1,443   157. 1,210   158. 1,625   159. 1,312   160. 810

161. 412   162. 1,145   163. 720   164. 1,620   165. 127

166. 1,235   167. 1,021   168. 1,030   169. 330   170. 120

171. 1,637   172. 1,013   173. 1,755   174. 1,514   175. 1,221

176. 1,313   177. 1,131   178. 1,430   179. 1,193   180. 534

181. 1,160   182. 1,322   183. 1,421   184. 1,140   185. 1,381

186. 1,420   187. 1,240   188. 1,110   189. 820   190. 1,360

191. 1,014   192. 1,120   193. 1,121   194. 1,120   195. 1,144

196. 1,413   197. 1,735   198. 1,640   199. 1,814   200. 1,493

Page 11: Subtraction with Regrouping

201. 448	202. 57	203. 184	204. 79	205. 319	206. 178
207. 687	208. 177	209. 188	210. 379	211. 289	212. 89
213. 59	214. 567	215. 486	216. 578	217. 137	218. 189
219. 87	220. 873	221. 88	222. 286	223. 75	224. 48
225. 189	226. 684	227. 86	228. 459	229. 69	230. 219
231. 38	232. 65	233. 149	234. 288	235. 189	236. 46
237. 59	238. 258	239. 75	240. 359	241. 569	242. 49
243. 158	244. 186	245. 319	246. 588	247. 228	248. 167
249. 385	250. 69	251. 136	252. 89	253. 488	254. 569
255. 189	256. 109	257. 187	258. 9	259. 55	260. 67
261. 324	262. 119	263. 589	264. 89	265. 18	266. 266
267. 16	268. 259	269. 185	270. 288	271. 689	272. 339
273. 269	274. 89	275. 35	276. 387	277. 89	278. 586
279. 586	280. 389	281. 389	282. 489	283. 57	284. 385
285. 559	286. 279	287. 649	288. 477	289. 159	290. 68
291. 589	292. 269	293. 79	294. 187	295. 79	296. 477
297. 239	298. 57	299. 165	300. 86	301. 485	302. 86
303. 179	304. 89	305. 89	306. 89	307. 86	308. 54
309. 142	310. 789	311. 739	312. 838	313. 466	314. 35
315. 179	316. 187	317. 587	318. 183	319. 38	320. 188

321. 89	322. 43	323. 85	324. 389	325. 387	326. 79
327. 144	328. 85	329. 42	330. 269	331. 344	332. 89
333. 365	334. 655	335. 169	336. 255	337. 389	338. 489
339. 179	340. 82	341. 279	342. 277	343. 489	344. 629
345. 86	346. 449	347. 78	348. 45	349. 521	350. 189
351. 77	352. 189	353. 85	354. 88	355. 49	356. 179
357. 549	358. 277	359. 18	360. 169	361. 28	362. 179
363. 89	364. 73	365. 79	366. 767	367. 589	368. 25
369. 666	370. 169	371. 486	372. 79	373. 184	374. 78
375. 439	376. 227	377. 87	378. 285	379. 222	380. 477
381. 269	382. 669	383. 285	384. 549	385. 89	386. 653
387. 89	388. 89	389. 177	390. 676	391. 577	392. 179
393. 88	394. 176	395. 54	396. 279		

Page 21: Make 1000

397. 917	398. 927	399. 990	400. 968	401. 928	402. 940
403. 910	404. 948	405. 972	406. 930	407. 913	408. 914
409. 932	410. 924	411. 989	412. 943	413. 925	414. 995
415. 933	416. 949	417. 965	418. 991	419. 957	420. 985
421. 936	422. 987	423. 983	424. 973	425. 934	426. 962
427. 920	428. 951	429. 977	430. 945	431. 974	432. 931
433. 941	434. 958	435. 937	436. 953	437. 918	438. 988

439. 993   440. 992   441. 956   442. 901   443. 911   444. 947

445. 982   446. 909

Page 24:   Matching the answers.

447. a.C b.D c.E d.B e.I f.F g.J h.G i.H j.A

448. a.H b.A c.D d.E e.G f.C g.J h.B i.I j.F

449. a.D b.F c.C d.B e.H f.I g.A h.E i.J j.G

450. a.E b.J c.G d.I e.B f.A g.F h.C i.H j.D

451. a.B b.H c.F d.I e.C f.E g.A h.G i.J j.D

452. a.B b.J c.C d.A e.I f.F g.D h.G i.H j.E

453. a.A b.B c.E d.H e.J f.D g.I h.C i.G j.F

454. a.E b.F c.I d.D e.J f.G g.B h.C i.H j.A

455. a.G b.I c.J d.C e.F f.H g.D h.E i.A j.B

456. a.J b.D c.F d.G e.B f.E g.H h.I i.A j.C

Page 34:   Addition Word Problems

457. 22   458. 21   459. 27   460. 15   461. 20   462. 27   463. 26

464. 18   465. 31   466. 18   467. 30   468. 12   469. 33   470. 20

471. 18   472. 6   473. 11   474. 11   475. 21   476. 33   477. 34

478. 11   479. 29   480. 19   481. 23   482. 9   483. 9   484. 11

485. 38   486. 23

Page 42:   Subtraction Word Problems

487. 4   488. 0   489. 3   490. 5   491. 1   492. 5   493. 16   494. 11

495. 6   496. 15   497. 6   498. 2   499. 1   500. 7   501. 4   502. 4

503. 14   504. 14   505. 3   506. 2   507. 8   508. 9   509. 3   510. 4

511. 3   512. 14   513. 10   514. 10   515. 3   516. 11   517. 0

Page 50: Addition Circles

518.

519.

520.

521.

522.

523.

524.

525.

526.

527.

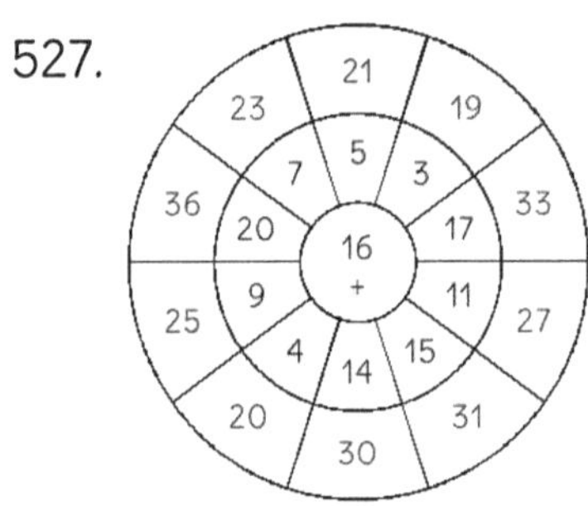

Page 55:   Circle Drills Subtraction

528.

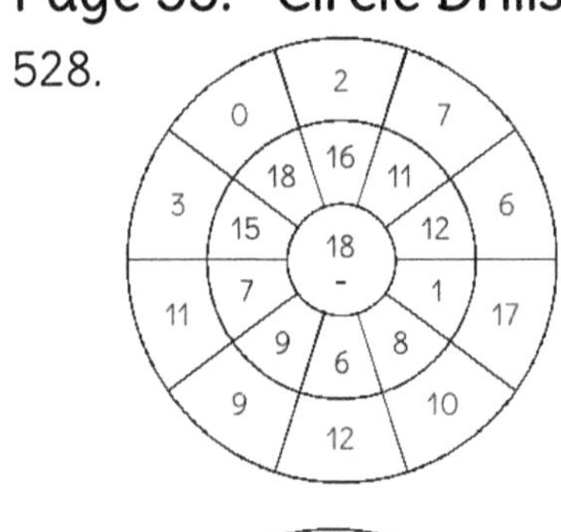

529.

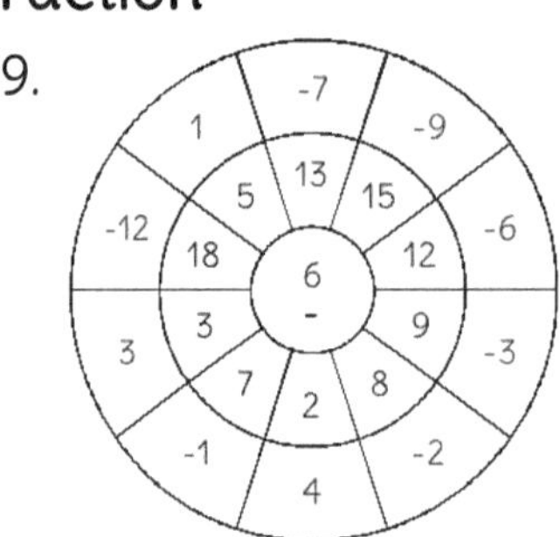

530.

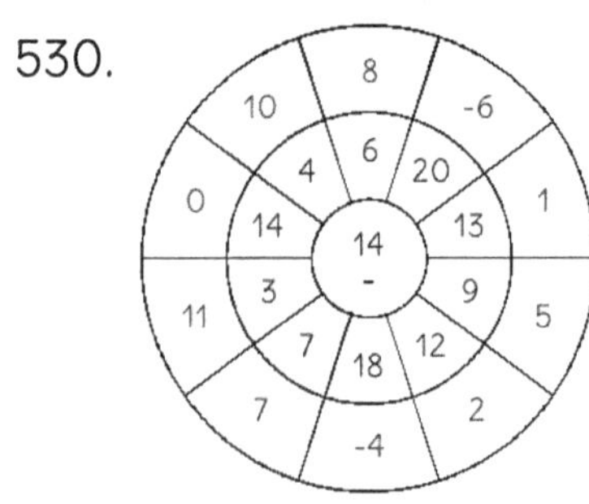

531.

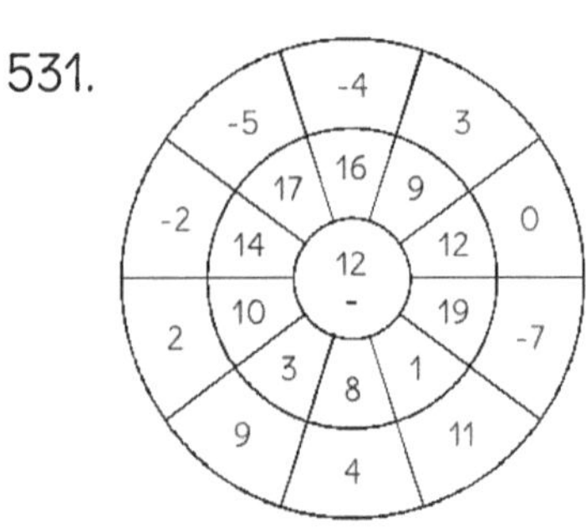

532.

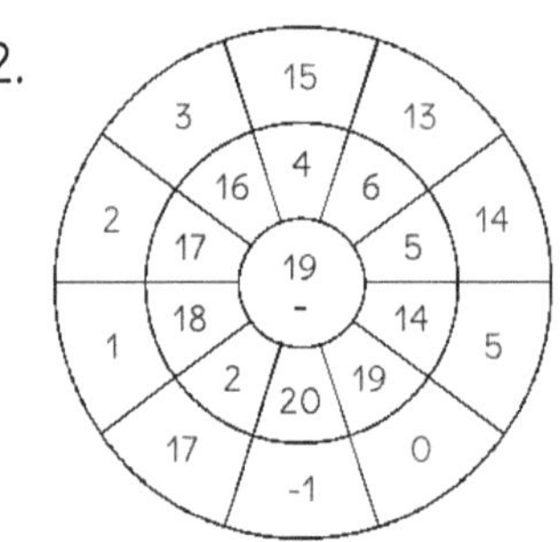

533.

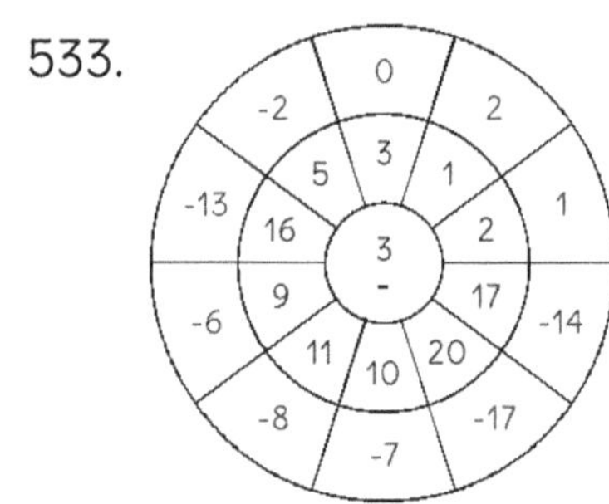

534.

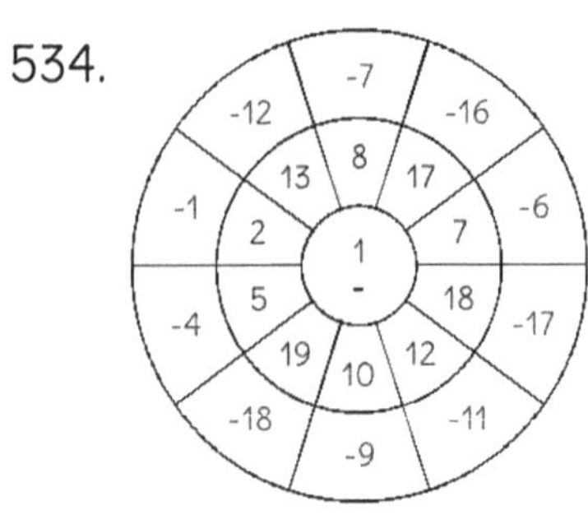

535.

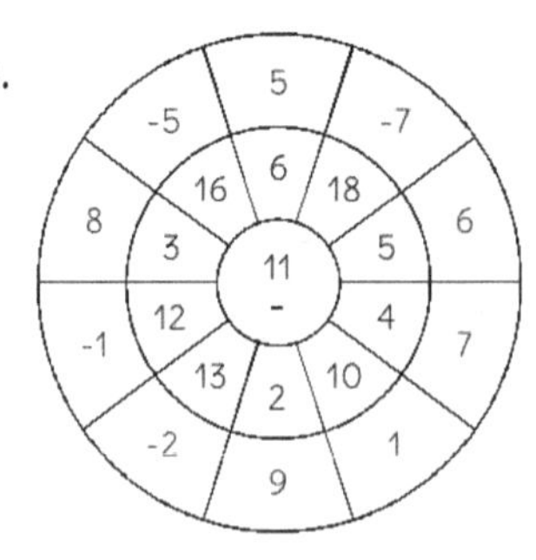

536.

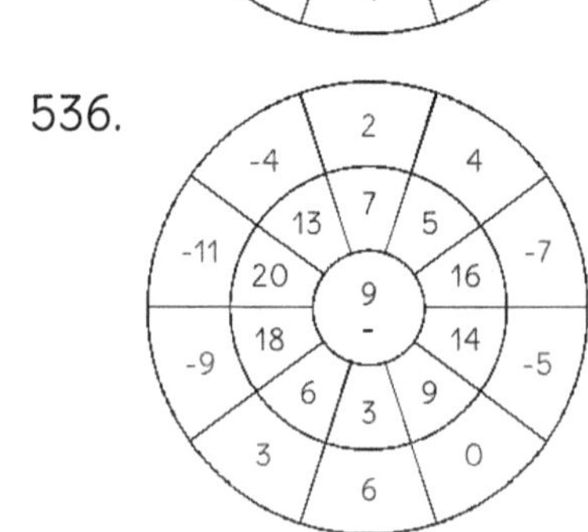

537.

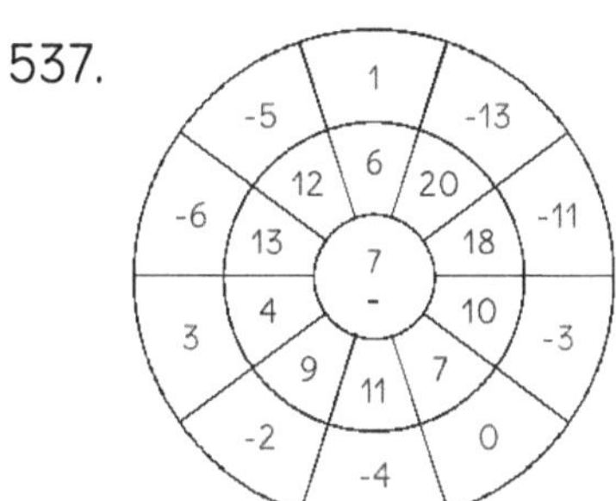